ADVANCE PR...

"I enjoyed reading through the huge catalogue of management mistakes that Marce Fernández has documented in order to set the stage for a clever proposal on how to make good decisions in situations that demand the best from us as executives in charge. I especially like the framework that invites us to apply knowledge, reflection and collaboration to the decision-making process. If business schools taught these types of concepts, we would see good decisions more often."

Bernardo García
Chief Financial & Administrative Officer, Alestra,
Monterrey, Mexico

"In the midst of our hypersonic world where machine-based intelligence increases the speed of all business transactions, errors made by human managers risk having even greater consequences than before. Competitors use AI to analyse your every move and will pounce in an instant. It's all the more reason to read *The Wrong Manager*. And watch out – failing to capture its learnings could be your big management mistake!"

Eric Stevenson
Vice President, Softbank Robotics, Paris, France

"I used to believe that the best decisions are simply the ones you make, because not making a decision means you will be left behind. *The Wrong Manager* takes this philosophy to a whole new level, showing how to ensure the decisions you make are, in fact, the right decisions. Essential reading in today's complex world."

Freddy Sharpe
Director, Climate Friendly Group, Sydney, Australia

"In an ever-faster changing world of uncertainty, all managers make mistakes – most take learnings from their mistakes, but only great managers can apply those learnings effectively to others in order to avoid them in the future. *The Wrong Manager* offers a succinct guide for the business manager to learn from others' mistakes without having to personally experience too many themselves, and that has to be good news for all concerned."

James Pitman
Managing Director for the UK & Europe, Study Group,
London, UK

"Running a successful organization is the art of making more right decisions than wrong ones and ensuring that the right decisions have the greatest impact. After reading *The Wrong Manager*, I have learned to make better decisions and get more things right, so I highly recommend it."

Rubén Ferreiro
Chief Executive Officer, VIKO Group, President,
Lanai Partners, Barcelona, Spain

"In my 30-year career as a financial services manager and entrepreneur, I have made many mistakes, although I was able to develop a fairly successful career. If I had had the opportunity to read *The Wrong Manager* several years ago, I would have avoided at least some of them. A very different perspective for a business book, which usually talks about success stories and not about mistakes; highly recommended for all those who want to improve their decision-making."

Stefano Calderano
Chief Executive Officer, Worldline Merchant Services Italia,
Rome, Italy

ACKNOWLEDGEMENTS

The 1992 MBA IMD Class,
which participated greatly in my research

The Latin Summit Group, for being always there
(the best WhatsApp group ever)

The IMD Alumni Club for their help and support

Shaymaa and Ephraim who helped me consult
the views of managers in Egypt and Kenya

María and Tim, who helped me share
the survey among young managers

My colleagues from Caixa Galicia,
from whom I learned so much

Craig, who helped me revise the text

Published by
LID Publishing
An imprint of LID Business Media Ltd.
LABS House, 15–19 Bloomsbury Way
London, WC1A 2TH, UK

info@lidpublishing.com
www.lidpublishing.com

A member of:

businesspublishersroundtable.com

Printed by Severn, Gloucester
ISBN: 978-1-911687-36-8
ISBN: 978-1-911687-37-5 (ebook)

Cover and page design: Caroline Li

MARCE FERNÁNDEZ

THE WRONG MANAGER

MANAGEMENT MISTAKES AND HOW TO AVOID THEM

MADRID | MEXICO CITY | LONDON
BUENOS AIRES | BOGOTA | SHANGHAI

CONTENTS

INTRODUCTION

There is a problem or situation; a goal is set; we get a mandate. As a consequence, a decision must be made. Then we tend to identify the alternatives, go through a process of analysis and finally make a choice. This is how *we believe* decision-making works. Sometimes we pick the right choice; sometimes we do not. History is full of poor decisions, although in the corporate world, how to differentiate between good and bad decisions does not seem so obvious. Who can determine if the choice made was the correct one? How can anybody be sure of having picked the best possible option? Are corporate decisions different from personal decisions? What is behind the frequent management mistakes? Are management errors all the same?

We might wonder if such questions make any sense. Managers and executives are better trained every year; studies and experiments – scientific or pseudoscientific – constantly offer enlightening conclusions about how our minds work and how the decision processes must operate to become truly effective. Old and emerging theories already make up a body of huge knowledge that seems to encompass all possible areas and fields about decision-making. What else can we do?

I have been working in the banking industry for almost 30 years, and about 10 doing strategic consulting. After 40 years of dealing with managers and executives, I feel their behaviour regarding decision-making has changed very little or not at all. I see how personal and professional goals are often confused, how particular issues frequently overlap with corporate objectives, how a lack of analysis underlies many decisions, how executives forget recommendations for sound management and even lose sight of the ultimate purpose of their positions over and over again. I see that mistakes are as present in corporate life as ever before.

Too many companies have had to shut down in the last decade, in the last year, surely yesterday. This is because managers and executives do not always make right decisions no matter how well trained they are, and sometimes no matter how long and diverse their experience is. Here are some examples I witnessed:

- A CEO talking about energy once – a basic, informal and superficial conversation – and suddenly picking up the phone to order the purchase of a large block of shares in an electric company.

- As an advisor of a company involved in diversifying activities, I attended a meeting to discuss the possible development of a software platform for football coaches. They reached an agreement, and we said our pleasant goodbyes. On the way back, we stopped for coffee and after 15 minutes of relaxed chat, the chairman of the company had a change of heart and decided to break the deal.

- The son of an executive told his father over breakfast that he had made a purchase from an online marketplace. So, this man walked into his office and the first thing he did was to reprimand his marketing and systems people because they did not have a marketplace like the competitor's. They were forced to drop all the projects they were working on to develop a marketplace that did not make sense (both platforms were shut down within two years, but nobody ever tried to find out what the problem had been).

These things happen all the time. I worked for more than 20 years in an industry that owned half of the banking business in Spain. The Savings Banks had undertaken a successful transformation process and become modern corporations capable of meeting the challenges of the financial markets, the technology, the declining margins and the overwhelming growth of their balance sheets. Their chairpersons and CEOs were regarded as social stars, people capable of moving the economy and also looking after social needs and caring for the culture and heritage around them. Everyone loved them as business partners, invited them to give lectures or for special occasions, and awarded them with the most unsuspected honours. The Spanish Savings Banks represented a history of pride, of things well done, of intelligence and, of course, success. But it all fell apart in just a few months. The industry vanished as if it had never existed. In less than a year, it lost its dominant market share in the most powerful industry in the country. All due to a long chain of decision mistakes made by exceptionally well-paid executives as well as auditors, financial rulers and political leaders.

As already mentioned, decision-making has been widely studied by the academic world. A quick review of decision theories shows us two different approaches: on one hand, normative/rational theories contend that decision makers always take the most logical choice when facing a complex problem or situation. According to them, decision makers take the option that *maximizes the result*. This approach tends to consider both personal characteristics and context as neutral factors in the decision process. On the other, we find some practical theories developed from the study of the real behaviour of decision makers and their cognitive performance. This practical approach takes into consideration the influence of the context, as well as the particular position of the decision makers. Therefore, it leaves room for errors to occur.

Although managers are a specific group of decision makers, the complex corporate environment in which they operate was barely taken into account by decision theories. As it was stated at the introduction of The Bradford Studies,[1] there was a gap (I believe there still is), an "absence of comparative empirical research on managerial decision-making." The Bradford project, however, put all its effort into analysing how big strategies are designed and implemented and not so much into how to make specific decisions in the face of specific managerial problems.

In her work on the capabilities required to become more competent at making decisions, Nadia Papamichail[2] reminds us of the various studies that "revealed that decision makers often take bad decisions (Janis, 1989), solve the wrong problem (Forrester, 2003) and cannot cope with uncertainty (Bazerman, 2002)." These circumstances bring heavy losses to the organizations every year. It is worth giving a twist to this. That is why I have written this book.

As an essential part of this work, I designed and carried out a survey (in Appendix 1) that was shared with managers and executives. Participants were asked to expose a management error that they were aware of and then answer a series of questions. Research findings are scattered throughout the book, supporting a given reasoning or showing alternative points of view. In Appendix 2, I list all the management errors described in the survey.

The 86 participants in the survey come from Argentina, Australia, Brazil, Egypt, Estonia, France, Germany, Italy, Kenya, Mexico, Singapore, Spain, Switzerland, the United Kingdom and the United States. The prototype of the respondent is a male executive over 45 years of age. Companies of different sizes are represented and 9.3% of those surveyed managers give an example involving public administration or nonprofit organizations. More than 25% of respondents are women and also 25.6% are under 45 (7% under 35).

Apart from the enlightening data it provided, the survey leaves us with another interesting finding: the reluctance of some managers and executives to admit mistakes, and not just in those specific cultures that tend to sweep matters under the carpet and avoid criticism. Many of the managers invited to participate refused to respond to the survey, claiming that their case did not match the questionnaire approach or that they were unable to figure out valid cases for the purpose of the research.

In the survey, 43 of the errors given as examples were made by top executives; 21 by politicians; 15 by the respondent's boss; 6 by a respondent's colleague; and 1, just one, was made by the respondent himself.

It was hardly surprising: after all, I already knew cognitive prejudices such as the *egocentric bias* that makes us recall the past in a self-serving manner, or the *confirmation bias* that inoculates us with the desire to be right. Willard V. Quine and J.S. Ullian[3] stated that confirmation bias blocks the progress of our knowledge. So we'd better get over it.

In this book I shall talk a little about cognitive biases, but no more than necessary. They are only one of the many underlying factors that explain management mistakes. By analysing the ultimate circumstances that prompted business errors, we will learn to avoid them and thus improve the results and the position of our organizations.

HOW TO APPLY DECISION THEORIES TO MANAGEMENT

Every decision starts because a change agent prompts it. The profit margin goes down, a new competitor enters your market, you need to hire someone, there is a clash with a partner, an event must be communicated ... A change agent means a break in the status quo. When faced with it, you can either stand back or you can act; that will be your first decision.

A decision is a choice but not a bet. A bet means to assign a key role to luck. You lay your chips where you *think*, where you *believe*, where you *feel* the ball will fall. By regarding a decision as a bet, we would be equating a company to a casino. A choice comes after an analysis and a (hopefully objective) comparison between options; a bet is an intuitive move based on random variables.

Gigerenzer and Gaissmaier[4] wondered: "How are decisions made?" And they also provided the response: "Three major answers have been proposed: the mind applies logic, statistics or heuristics." Decision-making theories developed from a practical approach arise from the combination of these three key concepts: logic as a form of reasoning consistent with the observed cause-effect relations; statistics as a way to interpret and verify those cause-effect relations through data; and heuristics as the mental processes that allow humans to make quick judgments based on their previous experiences.

2.1 LOGIC, STATISTICS, HEURISTICS ... AND RHETORIC

Logic is the *Logos* of the typical rhetorical triangle. It appeals directly to reasoning, to hard content, to the cause-effect relationship. Every manager is sure that they are capable of acting in harmony with logic, each person with a responsibility. I would say that everyone except satyrs believe that they act according to a more or less universal logic. However, *Logos* is not a stand-alone variable. Let's remember the rhetoric triangle: next to *Logos* in the other two vertices, we find *Ethos* (ethics, commitment, prestige, experience) and *Pathos* (feelings, beliefs, values, interests). Between *Logos* and *Pathos* there is usually a conflict. *Logos* tends to be considered a *neutral* concept but if *Pathos* wins out, then *Logos* loses its required neutrality.

You may have seen that video from February 2021[5] in which the US representative Lauren Boebert bragged about her right to carry a gun. She used two arguments in favour of her decision to carry a gun: she was willing to protect her four children by all means, and violence in US cities was extremely high. Lauren Boebert might not have thought about the reason behind the arguments she used. The danger to her children came from the people who took advantage of the right to carry a weapon in the United States and that right was precisely the main reason for the enormous number of firearm-related deaths in the US cities. Logic implies pragmatism, too; the wish to protect her children would require Mrs Boebert to be close to her children 24 hours a day, seven days a week, and her children were together at all times. It seems quite clear that Lauren Boebert's intention was not very realistic. Mrs Boebert seems to have performed counter-logical reasoning due to her deep feelings and beliefs.

> In the survey, 10 of the 86 respondents claimed that the decision of his or her example "made no sense."

Statistics is the second element required to make a decision, according to Gigerenzer and Gaissmaier. It measures the probability of success of an event and can tell us which option is more likely to meet the goal. In Mrs Boebert's example, we could ask which proportion of children shot in the United States in the last years could be defended by their mothers. We can use the compilation made by Brady United:[6] every year, around 7,957 children and teens are shot in the United States. Among those:

- 1,663 children and teens die from gun violence; 864 are murdered
- 6,294 children and teens survive gunshot injuries
- 662 die from gun suicide; 166 survive an attempted gun suicide
- 10 are killed by legal intervention; 101 are shot by legal intervention and survive
- 89 are killed unintentionally; 2,893 are shot unintentionally and survive
- 38 die, but the intent was unknown
- 380 survive being shot, but the intent was unknown

Looking at these figures, one may ask how many of those cases could have been avoided by an armed mother. We should also ask how many of those cases could be avoided by tighter gun control. By using statistics, it would be easy to conclude that Mrs Boebert's decision to carry a weapon may not be the best choice to reduce the number of children injured or killed by firearms.

Let's look at a more straightforward example (Figure 1): Imagine you have to go from A to B in an hour and you have to choose between two routes. Statistics can help you decide. Probabilities will tell you that, under the same conditions, you are more likely to arrive in time on Path 1.

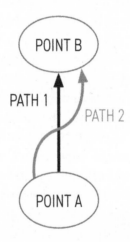

FIGURE 1: FROM POINT A TO POINT B

But other factors could enter the equation. In the middle of Path 1, there is a village where cars tend to stop about 10 to 15 minutes around 40% of the time. At least two days a week, traffic is really heavy on Path 1 and an accident occurs one day in ten; around 20% of those accidents are serious and require roadside assistance. Statistics will come to your aid to tell you on which route you are more likely to reach Point B on time.

The relationship between statistics and decision-making has been widely studied by the academic world. There are not too many cases in the business world where the odds of success or failure can be precisely determined. Management is the realm of uncertainty. The higher the uncertainty, the less accurate the statistics. On top of that, let's be honest: how many times have we seen managers making a decision after checking the odds of each option?

Heuristics can tell us: okay, I choose Path 2 because I have often travelled Path 2 and have always reached Point B on time. Heuristics are part of the behaviour of our brain, a kind of mechanism that allows us to make quick decisions or solve problems as soon as they arise. We resort to heuristics continuously, when our mind takes the shortcut to give an automatic response to a situation instead of reserving time and effort to analyse it and study the different alternatives from which we can choose. We take Herbert Simon's definition of heuristics[7] as the use of "experience to construct an expectation of how good a solution can be reasonably achieved." According to him, the "choice of heuristics is a function of the available knowledge of the decision maker and the characteristics of the situation in which a decision is made."

As a first approach to heuristics, we can say that, in many situations, it is not only useful but even unavoidable. Imagine we are driving again and approaching a traffic light that turns yellow. We do not have time to analyse the chances of crossing with no harm occurring. We decide in a fraction of a second whether we step on the accelerator or, on the contrary, we slow down and brake. There is no analysis in that important decision, just heuristics: a reaction based on past experiences.

However, there are situations in which heuristics can mislead us. Each time we face a new situation, our mind will tend to draw to our attention a previous one as if it were similar but may not be so alike. Those differences our mind hides from us can cause a wrong assessment and, therefore, a poor decision. The so-called cognitive biases make our own brain trick us. Its intention is to work out the problem through a quick evaluation and that may lead to a hasty decision.

There are cases that leave little room for doubt: complex situations that require not only the consideration and evaluation of multiple inputs of a different kind but also some supplementary and specialized participation. If context varies from our previous experience, if the industry is different, if the new organization has nothing to do with the old one, it does not seem advisable to be guided mainly by heuristics. In mistake number 31, one of the respondents of our survey gives a good example of the incorrect use of heuristics.

31 | A new CEO was hired. He came from another company and replicated the same management model despite the great differences between the two organizations.

Heuristics has something to do with the *Ethos* of the rhetoric theory. *Ethos*, considered as ethics, values and arguments, is used to build credibility. Heuristics, understood as the abilities developed through the track record and experience, contributes to the growth of reputation. Why do we insist on the parallelism between decision-making and rhetoric? First of all, because "Decision makers are simultaneously speakers and listeners when they seek to construct and deploy resources that justify their choice" (Hoefer & Green Jr, 2016).[8] Rhetoric, as a function of deliberation under a context of uncertainty and integrating *Logos* (logic), *Ethos* (values) and *Pathos* (emotion), may be considered a useful theory of choice in human affairs. If we admit the emotional factor has a relevant influence on decision-making, rhetoric gives us that concept of *Pathos*. In some way, rhetoric reaffirms the validity of decisions as a concept that rejects systematization, a concept subject to the influence of emotions. As Carolyn Miller[9] reminds us, Aristotle speaks of rhetoric as "things about which we deliberate, but for which we do not have systematic rules."

And I call upon rhetoric because a decision is not just a one-moment move. Instead, it is a trigger-point move. A decision starts a series of actions, the first of which is communication. It is an exercise built on making a decision and the transmission of that decision. After being made, the decision must be properly communicated for implementation. The listeners become the recipients of the decision and their point of view, their thoughts and also their feelings must be taken into account.

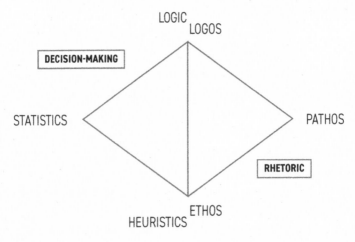

FIGURE 2: DECISION-MAKING AND RHETORIC DIAGRAM

Let's see a practical example of what we have just outlined in this section. Imagine you are enjoying your holiday. You plan to travel in a certain region and have rented a car online. Once you are at the counter to collect the keys, the assistant asks you: do you want fully comprehensive insurance? The decision will very much depend on the balance among the previous key factors:

FACTOR	POSSIBLE DECISION
Statistics	You estimate how many trips you will make in your life and how much the fully comprehensive insurance would cost. Now you need the average probability of an accident, which is a public figure. You can even correct that number by applying your driving style. If the probability of an accident multiplied by the average cost of repairing a car is greater than the accumulated insurance cost, you must buy the insurance; otherwise, you should not.
Logic/Logos	You would reason: if I want to have a carefree holiday, I will not be worried about a possible car accident; the best way is to buy a fully comprehensive policy.
Heuristics/Ethos	You could think: I have never had a single scratch on my previous trips, so there is no reason to fear an accident on this one; and you will reject the agent's proposal.
Pathos (emotions)	If you feel secure enough, you will decline supplementary insurance; if you have more doubts, you may buy it.

The question will be now: where is the optimal balance? Decision theories have tried to sort this out for us.

2.2 A QUICK REVIEW OF DECISION THEORIES

Researchers and scientists have spent a great deal of effort and time in analysing and trying to model how we make decisions. Microeconomics, statistics, operations research, cost-benefit analysis, risk analysis, artificial intelligence, computer science simulation, cognitive and social psychology, etc.: the vast knowledge stored in all these disciplines and some others has been put at the service of decision theorists who have proposed their studies and conclusions to the academic world. Many of those studies have proven useful in such diverse fields as public health, the environment, military strategy and advertising. Are they also helpful in management? I intend to answer that question in this section.

Decision science tries to identify the elements that make up complex decision problems so that a set of valid logical axioms can be obtained to compare alternatives, one of which will emerge as the optimal choice. The analysis should produce a quantitative utility function from which to assign a comparative utility to each option. The values for a set of options can be used to rank decision makers' preferences.

All good if it were not for the fact that, in some terms, decision science studies and models how decisions *should be taken* rather than how they are actually made.

In the field of economics, the positive theory assumes that all the agents of a market pursue maximum utility, so they will carry out the same cost-benefit analysis to obtain the best result in any scenario. As Amos Tversky and Daniel Kahneman[10] stated as early as in 1989, this theory "was conceived as a normative model of an idealized decision maker, not as a description of the behaviour of real people ... We argue that the deviations of actual behaviour from the normative model are too widespread to be ignored, too systematic to be dismissed as random error and too fundamental to be accommodated by relaxing normative systems." A perfectly rational behaviour implies an optimum use of logic and statistics.

But, as we should know, the perfect world does not exist, nor does the perfect decision maker. Two well-trained and experienced managers can make the opposite decision on the same problem. As Derek Pugh and David Hickson pointed out,[11] "Managers have to make effective decisions to keep the organization flourishing. As long as there is management, there will be the problem of how to manage better. In one sense, attempts at answers to this problem will be as numerous as managers, for each will bring an individual approach to the task."

> In the survey, 52.3% of the participants thought that "The personality of the decision maker" was fairly important or absolutely critical to make a good decision; and 44.2% also agreed that "The mood and state of mind of the decision maker" was fairly important or critical.

The simple observation of reality disproves the conclusions of the positive theory, as many professors have tended to discuss over the last decades. As Campitelli and Gobet pointed out in an aforementioned article, "Tversky and Kahneman agreed with (Herbert) Simon that economic agents are not perfectly rational." They highlight Simon's contribution to the study of decision-making by showing his strong criticism of perfect rationality and proposing instead the so-called 'bounded rationality.' He understands that the capacity of the human mind for analysing and solving complex problems is very small compared with the size of those problems to be solved by objectively rational behaviour. According to this, the weaknesses of the human cognitive system and the limitations in accessing relevant information do not allow people to make perfectly rational decisions. Campitelli and Gobet recall Simon's conclusions: "People have an adequacy criterion to decide whether an alternative is satisfactory, and that they choose the first option that fulfils this criterion. Hence, people do not evaluate all the available options, and they do not carry out a full cost-benefit analysis of the possible options." Herbert Simon concludes that people try to choose a 'good enough' option, not the best one, and shows that the decision criteria vary based on the following factors:

- the level of expertise of the decision maker
- the characteristics of the environment
- the attributes of the task at hand
- the current state of search in which information plays a key role

In the survey, 95.3% of the participants thought that "The experience of the decision maker" was fairly important or absolutely
critical to make a good decision; and 90.7% also agreed that
"Being able to understand the context affecting the decision" was
fairly important or even critical.

Tversky and Kahneman expanded the psychological
approach to decision-making and made it widely known.
Through their theory of 'biased rationality,' they proved
that humans are conditioned by their previous experiences
as decision makers and also by some contextual factors
such as the way the problems are framed. To Kahneman
and Tversky, any person makes decisions through heuristic
processes and, therefore, is influenced by his or her own
prejudices (biases), which may distort the evaluation of the
options and the weighting of success probabilities.

Their 'prospect theory'[12] is a good example of how the
human mind can make a person choose not the best option
in terms of utility. According to the prospect theory, people tend to overweigh the chances of loss compared to an
equivalent probability of making a similar profit. Hence
people tend to behave in a risk-averse way when dealing
with a choice leading to gains and in a risk-seeking way
when facing a choice leading to losses. This conclusion
totally contradicts the essence of the positive theory.

In the survey, only 19.8% of the participants stated that "The
influence of cognitive biases was not a reason at all" for the
management mistake they gave as an example; in fact, 54.7% of
respondents thought that cognitive biases "had a relevant effect"
or "was the main or one of the main reasons" for the management
error in their example.

Another critical contribution to decision-making from Daniel Kahneman's is his 'System 1, System 2 theory,'[13] according to which decision makers have two levels of reasoning: System 1 uses heuristic processes for fast, automatic and belief-based decisions, whereas System 2 uses an analytic reasoning for slow, sequential and deducted decisions. We shall see the relevance of the so-called 'dual theory' for management a little later in the section.

Gary Klein[14] developed the naturalistic decision-making approach that implied a step beyond the preceding works. As he states at the beginning of *Sources of Power*, his book was written to balance the existing theories and takes a different perspective. "I document human strengths and capabilities that typically have been downplayed or even ignored," he states in the Introduction. Somehow, Klein feels the experience and knowledge of decision makers were not properly assessed. He studies the real-world context of decisions and focuses his research on difficult decisions made by experts under time pressure. He concludes that the sources of power required in natural environments are not any analytical processes but the previous experience of decision makers.

Klein makes a statement that undermines the importance of the analysis and highlights experience and intuition instead: "The challenge is to identify how that experience came into play. The conventional sources of power include deductive logical thinking, analysis of probabilities and statistical methods. Yet the sources of power that are needed in natural settings are usually not analytical at all. The power of intuition enables us to size up a situation quickly. The power of mental simulation lets us imagine how a course of action might be carried out. The power of metaphor lets us draw on our experience by suggesting parallels between the current situation and something else we have come across. The power of storytelling helps us consolidate our experiences to make them available in the future."

To some extent, Britta Herbig and Andreas Glöckner[15] try to qualify Klein's model when they propose the use of Parallel Constraint Satisfaction theory (PCS) to study the influence of expertise in decision-making. According to this theory, decisions are made following two processes. Through the first one – the automatic consistency-maximizing process in the primary network – the decision makers can quickly handle a large amount of information and so are able to work out most of the problems they must face. The second network implies a longer and more deliberate process in which the decision makers use different tools, such as statistics. According to these authors, "Deliberate processes (i.e. conscious reflection) are only employed if an adequate, good interpretation regarding the importance of a situation cannot be found. That is, deliberate processes are activated if the consistency of a resulting mental representation is below a threshold." Leaving apart ambiguous concepts as 'consistency' or 'threshold,' it seems quite obvious that the PCS theory implies another version of the 'dual theories.'

The dual theories of reasoning were studied in depth by Jonathan Evans in his article "Dual-Processing Accounts of Reasoning, Judgment and Social Cognition."[16] In the following table, I highlight some of the features he identifies of both systems or levels of reasoning, which I will analyse in greater depth in section 2.3:

SYSTEM 1	SYSTEM 2
Unconscious	Conscious
Automatic	Controlled
Low effort	High effort
Rapid	Slow
Holistic, perceptual	Analytic, reflective
Associative	Rule based
Domain specific	Domain general
Pragmatic	Logical
Parallel	Sequential

Finally, Richard Thaler follows Kahneman's line of work[17] and studies new aspects of behavioural economics linked, above all, to consumer decisions. He coins the term 'nudge'[18] to describe the rational changes the consumers must undergo to optimize their decisions and overcome the mental shortcuts typical of decision makers. Thaler's main contributions to decision-making were in the field of 'financial behaviour,' where he proved the bounded rationality of people in making financial decisions. He applied the concept of 'mental accounting'[19] to summarize the wide variety of biases that affect people when they face their financial choices.

2.3 ARE DECISION THEORIES APPLICABLE TO MANAGEMENT?

Firstly, we should ask: What is actually a management decision? Well, it is a decision made by a manager. So here it comes the new obvious question: What does a manager do? I have gone through the literature and the answers do not seem that obvious. It is not my intention to take too long on this or to deviate from the purpose of the book. So I shall confine myself to pointing out a few basic guidelines: On one hand, Herbert Simon's approach according to whom management is an equivalent of decision-making and the managers must try to make effective decisions; that is their role. On the other, we see many other authors who follow the path defined by Henry Fayol, who stated[20] that "Management is to forecast, to plan, to organize, to command, to coordinate and control activities of others."

Fayol's studies, although dated, are quite interesting and confirm that management has not changed so much over time. As Derek Pugh and David Hickson remind us, "For Fayol (1841–1925), managing means looking ahead, which makes the first factor – the process of forecasting and planning – a central business activity. Management must 'assess the future and make provision for it.' To function adequately, a business organization needs a plan that has the characteristics of 'unity, continuity, flexibility and precision.' The problems of planning that management must overcome are (a) making sure the objectives of each part of the organization are securely welded together (unity), (b) using both short- and long-term forecasting (continuity), (c) being able to adapt the plan in the light of changing circumstances (flexibility), and (d) attempting to accurately predict courses of action (precision). The essence of planning is to allow the optimum use of resources."

Peter Drucker somehow brings together the above perspectives and highlights two powerful ideas: managers always have to think of the impact of a decision on the present, the short-term future, and the long-term future; and, according to his famous quote, "There is nothing so useless as doing efficiently that which should not be done at all." In other words: a manager must understand what must be done.

If we try to summarize the three previous approaches, we come to the conclusion that the main role of the managers is to make effective decisions both for the short and for the long run; let's remember that 'effectiveness' means the ability to meet a goal. The first objective of any organization is to ensure its long-term survival, which means consolidating its position in the future. To do this, managers must handle complex scenarios and not simply solve immediate problems; we will return to this distinction in a moment.

Following the so-called VUCA context[21], we can describe the scenario in which managers perform as:

- Volatile: the context changes unexpectedly and it is difficult to foresee the duration of the changes
- Uncertain: the situation involves many factors to be considered and some may not be known; uncertainty

also affects the information to be handled, which can be either scarce or brutally excessive

- Complex: most of the factors involved interact with each other; new areas of expertise are required, especially those linked to technology
- Ambiguous: the cause-effect relationships are not clear at all, which makes the analysis more intricate; sometimes, the final goal is not obvious either

We could add some other relevant characteristics about the context where management decisions are made:

- High-risk consequences: the impact of the choice to make may be quite significant
- Dual perspective: those consequences may affect both the organization and the decision maker as an individual
- Unlimited alternatives: decisions are no longer straightforward. Now the alternatives before a problem or situation are all that the decision maker can figure out, each one with its own set of uncertainties
- Interpersonal issues: it is not only the logic and emotions of the decision maker that must be taken into account, but also those of the people affected by the decision

Let's see whether the conditions of the experiments carried out to establish the decision theories entirely fulfil the features of the management decision context we have just described:

1. The theories were established by eminent professors after careful laboratory tests. Except for Klein's research, the tests were carried out through ad-hoc

exercises rather than checking the real world. But as already referred, Klein focused on specific conditions: expert decision makers under extreme time pressure. His prospects were firefighters, military leaders, pilots, nurses, nuclear power plant operators or chess masters, never managers.

2. The subjects of the decision studies used to be (again, except Klein's) inexperienced people placed in an artificial scenario. But managers tend to be expert people working in natural scenarios.

3. The goals of the tests were usually crystal clear, just the opposite of what occurs in the business arena, where defining a goal does not seem that straightforward.

4. The tests carried out in the studies also used to be simple tasks from which general conclusions were obtained. But management decisions tend to imply complex choices to make in quite difficult contexts.

5. The conclusions of the studies were reached by the professors in charge of the research. There were not external observers or expert managers attending the experiments and projecting the conclusions to the corporate environment.

6. The tests used proposed two answers: one right, one wrong. The participant would choose between them. But in the corporate universe, the answers tend to be a range of alternatives. In fact, one of the keys of a right choice could be the finding of an innovative – not so easy to be aware of – solution to the problem.

7. In most of the studies, competition was not part of the tests, nor was the reaction of a counterpart, both key elements for the outcome of management decisions.

8. Most of the tests implied a far shorter time span than the time periods that managers usually work with (or should work with).

9. Finally, the research projects normally use a rock-hard concept of decision-making. They hardly manage different types of decisions which, as we will see, may make a real difference to assess the quality of the choice.

The conclusion of the previous nine points is that decision theories do not allow a crude application to management. The theories should be considered as general references of human behaviour – a decision implies a behaviour and managers are human, right? – but not as conclusions that can be directly transferred to management activity. The conditions in which most of the research was carried out lie far from the conditions in which managers operate: managers cannot free themselves from their human nature when making decisions, so they are as exposed to personal limitations as other people.

System 1 and System 2 are great examples of how decision theories can be tailored to managers' activity. In a preceding statement in this section, I concluded that the role of managers is not to work out immediate tasks but to improve the overall position of their organizations. I cannot easily see how System 1 could be applied in this context. The conditions under which managers make decisions constrain their ability to operate according to the conditions of System 1.

In the survey, only 15.1% of the participants thought that important decisions in an organization are made "Quickly, just when
the decision maker understands the situation." In fact, just a tiny
4.7% of the respondents think that the important decisions should
be made "Quickly ... ; there is no time to waste."

Experiments carried out by Ap Dijksterhuis[22] made a relevant contribution in this regard. Ap Dijksterhuis found
out what he called 'the unconscious thought,' which he
describes as a powerful way of thinking that combines both
conscious and unconscious abilities. Unconscious thought
would work like this: there is a problem to be solved; once
the decision maker understands it, they ignore it consciously for a while; after that, they come back to the problem with the solution brought by their mind. This process
was analysed and confirmed by quite a few studies, which
showed the unconscious system keeps on thinking about
an issue even in the absence of any conscious dedication.

According to Dijksterhuis' experiments, "When making
complex decisions, a brief period of unconscious thought
will lead to a better decision relative to conditions under
which unconscious thought is prevented." He explains
this in terms of the difficulties of the conscious system in
being able to manage a large amount of information in a
relatively short period of time; therefore, the representation
of this information in the mind is likely to be disorganized.
Through unconscious thought, the individual pieces of
information are associated and integrated, making them a
clearer and more manageable set of information in memory.

The experiments carried out by Professor Dijksterhuis
show some limitations when applied directly to a management context. The participants were college students, not
managers; they had to choose among a certain number of

given alternatives; and they had to answer with no time available for any basic calculation (criteria weighing, for example). Though it would be risky to transfer their conclusions to the field of management decisions, unconscious thinking opens a useful intermediate level between System 1 and System 2 of the 'dual theory.'

If System 1 means a quick, automated reasoning and System 2 means a slow and reflexive reasoning, the "In-between System" would be a combination of the automatic and the reflexive thinking according to the chart below.

SYSTEM 1	IN-BETWEEN SYSTEM	SYSTEM 2
Unconscious	Unconscious thought	Conscious
Automatic	Not so automatic	Controlled
Low effort	Not so low effort	High effort
Rapid	Needs a while	Slow
Holistic, perceptual	Quickly reflective	Analytic, reflective
Associative	Experience based	Rule based
Domain specific	Rather specific domain	Domain general
Pragmatic	Both pragmatic and logical	Logical
Parallel	Short chain of sequences	Sequential

Therefore, unconscious thought is not as fully automatic as System 1 is, requires a little effort and takes some time to function properly. It also triggers the association of ideas, but this will partly depend on the level of expertise of the decision maker on a specific domain.[23] It tends to apply a pragmatic approach but with a certain dose of logic. Finally, though it is sequential[24] like System 2, the sequence chain is rather short.

The description of the 'In-between System' would not be complete unless we add two other considerations. As Ap Dijksterhuis stated, "Making sound decisions requires integration of large amounts of information into impressions and a comparison between these impressions to arrive at a preference. To do this, two things are required. One needs enough processing capacity to deal with large amounts of information, and one needs skills sophisticated enough to integrate information in a meaningful and accurate way." Through unconscious thinking, decision makers are able to deal with a large amount of information. They are also able to imagine new solutions different from the more obvious ones that were shown as soon as the problem was exposed. Thus, alternatives and Information are two key elements when defining the role of the thinking systems.

SYSTEM	ALTERNATIVES	USE OF INFORMATION
System 1	Association between one problem and one solution	Mainly heuristics from a few pieces of Information
In-between System	Unconscious comparison among a few set of alternatives	Unconscious selection of the key Information
System 2	Analysis of a wide set of possible alternatives	Comprehensive use of Information; calculation if needed

The existence of this intermediate System in management decisions was confirmed in the survey, as it can be inferred from the data below.

- Question number 4: How do you think the decision in your example was made?
- Question number 7: How do you think important decisions of an organization should be made?
- Question number 8: How do you think most of the important decisions of an organization are actually made?

For each question, there were four possible answers:

a. Quickly, once the decision maker understands the situation
b. After a short period of reflection based on one's own experience and after checking the key information
c. After a thorough process of analysis considering all the factors involved in the situation
d. After a thorough process of analysis and in agreement with the colleagues with a competent word in the situation

And the results were as follow:

QUESTIONS/ANSWERS	QUICKLY	AFTER SHORT REFLECTION	THOROUGH ANALYSIS	THOROUGH AND COLLECTIVE
Q4: How was it in the example?	21	35	9	21
Q7: How should it be?	4	4	20	58
Q8: How is it normally?	13	42	16	15

While most managers and executives believe that decisions need to be made after thorough analysis and collective discussion, they are actually taken after a short period of reflection as Ap Dijksterhuis suggests. In fact, answer "b" was the preferred option in Q4 and Q8 by far.

MANAGERS MAKE MISTAKES ALL THE TIME

Making decisions is the main activity of any manager or professional and is also one of the main tasks of a politician. It is something we do all the time. Decisions of different kinds, scope and relevance; simple or complex decisions; individual or collective decisions. It is what we have prepared for. It is what we aspire to. It is what they expect from us. However, we often feel confused and hesitant before a decision. It is not easy to decide.

At the end of the day, any decision is a personal move. You can get news, data, reports, advice, opinions, but the final decision is yours, something you do on your own. You are responsible for your decisions, and you cannot anticipate their outcome. After any decision you make, there is just uncertainty. The decision method you use, consciously or unconsciously, should try to reduce this uncertainty.

Charles Munger referred to the vulnerability of decision makers at a well-known conference[25] over 20 years ago. Daniel Kahneman and Amos Tversky demonstrated through their meticulous studies that the human mind could not be considered reliable under uncertainty. We know that we cannot trust our minds, our intuition, or even our experience. Despite this, we continue to make decisions without observing a proper method. And we keep on making the same mistakes over and over.

We accept the mistakes of managers just as we admit traffic accidents. If the automobile sector had developed on the basis of security as the first decision criterion, there would not be a million deaths each year on the roads. In the same way, if an adequate decision system were implemented in companies, there would not be so many serious mistakes in the history of management.

Because leaders are not superheroes. Regardless of how much they earn or how much attention they receive from the media, at the end of the day, they are regular people, women and men with their shortcomings and weaknesses. More or less gifted, more or less qualified, they suffer the usual human constraints. They make mistakes just like the rest of humankind. And do you know what? Despite all we have heard about learning from our mistakes, we tend to repeat them over and over.[26]

It is the right moment in this book to recall a historical error – or rather a historical chain of errors – with tragic consequences.

THE LESSONS OF THE TITANIC

The Royal Mail Ship Titanic[27] sank in the early hours of April 15, 1912, off the coast of Newfoundland in the North Atlantic after laterally striking an iceberg during its maiden voyage. Of the 2,240 passengers and crew on board, more than 1,500 lost their lives in the disaster. Stiff competition between the two major shipping companies in the first half of the 20th century made a project like the Titanic possible. The battle in the steam engine industry was fought between the White Star Line and the Cunard. Cunard already had two of the most sophisticated and luxurious ships of its time.

After Cunard presented its ocean liners, J. Bruce Ismay, CEO of White Star, struck a deal with William J. Pirrie, president of Harland and Wolff, to build three large ships. In fact, they conceived the *Olympic Class* ocean liners during a dinner party. As part of the new class of ocean liners, each ship would measure 882 feet long and 92.5 feet at its widest, making them by far the largest of their time. In March 1909, the construction of the Titanic began at the Harland and Wolff shipyard in Belfast.

The work lasted for two hectic years. Every aspect of the project was a challenge either because of technological requirements or procurement constraints. The board had to deal with all sorts of serious problems and was said to have been in permanent crisis mode. With the eyes of the world on the Titanic, the purpose was to complete the project on time and overcome any unexpected situation that could arise. Innovative solutions, larger amounts of material and more workers than anticipated were required.

Olympic Class was really big, which demanded new approaches and compromises. The Titanic and her sister ships used three normal-size docks. Their innovative triple-screw propellers created a hazard for other ships. Each of the great ships required three million rivets that acted like glue to hold everything together. The builder of the Titanic struggled to obtain enough good rivets and riveters and ultimately settled on faulty materials that may have doomed the ship. The Titanic had three functional funnels: the fourth was purely aesthetic to make the ship look more imposing. Thomas Andrew's original design was conceived with only three funnels, but White Star thought a ship of such grandeur needed to display four.

Captain Edward Smith was appointed to command the ship. Throughout his career, Smith earned a reputation for being popular with both crew and passengers. In fact, he was nicknamed 'the millionaire's Captain' because he was so loved by wealthy travellers. After the Titanic's maiden voyage, Captain Smith was supposed to retire. He also had unquestionable experience commanding especially large ships. However, Smith's career was peppered with major setbacks. For example, in 1911 the *Olympic* under his command was severely damaged in a collision with the British cruiser *Hawke*. Some of Smith's ships ran aground.

Although no career is without its setbacks, so Smith's reputation as a captain was not tarnished by these events. Was Captain Smith the right man to command the Titanic? That is still a matter of debate.

The Titanic's departure from Southampton was scheduled for April 10. In preparation for the manoeuvre, a small coal fire was found in one of its bunkers, which the firemen hosed down. The captain and the chief engineer considered that the fire was unlikely to cause any structural damage to the hull, so the firemen were ordered to finish extinguishing the fire at sea. Some experts thought that the fire became uncontrollable, forcing a full-speed crossing. At such a pace, the collision with the iceberg could not be avoided.

After four days of sailing, the Titanic received some reports of ice from other ships. On April 14, around 11.30pm, a lookout raised the alarm about a nearby iceberg on the ship's route. The engines immediately reversed, and the ship turned sharply to avoid direct impact. However, the Titanic skimmed the side of the iceberg, scattering chunks of ice on the foredeck. Was it the most appropriate manoeuvre in those circumstances? Many doubt it.

After the scare, the Titanic continued the journey. No one knew that the iceberg had cut a 300-foot slit in the hull below the waterline. By the time the captain toured the damaged area with Thomas Andrews of Harland and Wolff, five compartments were already flooding, and the bow of the ship was tilting downward. Andrews mistakenly reckoned that the Titanic might remain afloat for only an hour and a half, and the captain ordered the lifeboats to be loaded. Then a chaotic evacuation began. Most boats, with room for 65 persons, were launched with far fewer people, some even with a small number of passengers.

The builders of the Titanic believed they had created an unsinkable ship. This same overconfidence explains the brutal impact the sinking of the Titanic had on the public. Five detailed investigations took place on both sides of the Atlantic, which led to multiple interviews with passengers and maritime experts. Every aspect was scrutinized, in particular the conduct of the officers and crew and the construction elements of the ship. The reports produced after these arduous processes were not always conclusive.

According to some hypotheses, the Titanic was doomed from the beginning precisely because of a design that had been presented as a great technological breakthrough. The *Olympic*-class liners featured a double bottom and 15 watertight bulkhead compartments equipped with watertight and power doors that could be operated remotely from the ship's bridge. But the design of the watertight compartment contained a flaw that turned out to be a critical factor: while the individual bulkheads were actually watertight, the walls separating the bulkheads extended only a few feet above the waterline, so the water could flow from one compartment to another, especially once the ship started to tilt.

Regarding the ship's speed, the narrative that the accident could have been averted had the Titanic not been travelling too fast, if the captain had slowed the pace, finally prevailed. One of the conclusions of the investigation into the accident included this sentence: "The evidence shows that he – the Captain – was not trying to make any record passage or indeed any exceptionally quick passage. He was not trying to please anybody but was exercising his own discretion in the way he thought best. He made a mistake, a very grievous mistake, but one in which, in face of the practice and of past experience, negligence cannot be said to have had any part; and in the absence of negligence, it is, in my opinion, impossible to fix Captain Smith with blame."

The ocean liner could also have sunk because poor-quality rivets were used. They could not withstand the pressure and let tons of ice-cold seawater in. Some scientists said the problems started when the ambitious construction plan forced Harland and Wolff to go beyond their usual rivet suppliers and include smaller forgings.

Another critical safety mistake that contributed to the loss of so many lives was the inadequate number of lifeboats. The Titanic could carry 2,435 passengers and had a crew of approximately 900, making a total of approximately 3,300 potential travellers. However, it only had 20 lifeboats, which could hold a maximum of 1,178 people.

The Titanic's was a landmark disaster brought on by a string of professional and managerial mistakes. By reviewing the previous paragraphs, we can identify some of them:

1. The setting of the goal. The Titanic was built primarily to make an impression on the society of that time and to brag about being the flagship of the most avant-garde corporation. This meant that luxury prevailed over security and efficiency.

2. The whole project was dominated by an excess of confidence. The ship was deemed unsinkable, so no evacuation drills were conducted, and no sufficient lifeboats were provided. Also, the charcoal fire was not considered enough of a problem to postpone the departure.

3. The scale of the challenge was so great that many technical problems could not be properly worked out, such as the effect of the size of the ship, the building of the watertight bulkhead compartments or the quality of the rivets.

4. The profile of the captain who commanded the ocean liner could suggest that the selection had not been based on the most adequate criteria.

5. Some navigation decisions did not help to avoid the tragedy, such as the apparently excessive speed, not stopping when they were aware of the ice in the area and the manoeuvre to avoid a direct impact with the iceberg.

6. Finally, there is consensus on the terrible evacuation management that took place after the accident.

If the consequences of human error turn out to be tragic, they cause, as did the sinking of the Titanic, our confidence to collapse and show us more than ever that we are fallible beings subject to weakness and error despite our frequent vanity and hubris.

3.2 DIFFERENT TYPES OF MISTAKES

In 1970, Stephan Wozniak worked at Hewlett Packard as a computer engineer. In his spare time, he created a small computer that he presented to the HP CEO, who failed to see its market potential. Wozniak continued to develop his invention, which he presented to the board of HP on several further occasions. Finally, he gave up and quit. With Steve Jobs, he founded Apple. Its first product was Apple I, Woz's invention. There can be little doubt as to the huge mistake made by Hewlett Packard's board, and its enormous consequences.

In 1975, Pepsi launched the 'Pepsi Challenge' campaign, consisting of a taste-off between Pepsi and Coke. Most consumers preferred Pepsi. The campaign implied a drastic drop in Coke consumption. So, Coca-Cola decided to change its formula to align it with the taste of Pepsi, which turned out to be a disaster. It sparked a wave of protests from its consumers, and the company had to immediately back down. That formula change by Coca-Cola seems to be another undoubtedly serious error of management (which they eventually turned around).

Let's jump ahead a few years to 1993, when John Meriwether, former vice president and director of bond trading at Salomon Brothers, created Long Term Capital Management (LTCM), a hedge fund for which he hired two Nobel laureates and a former vice president of the Federal Reserve. They gave high returns in their first years and became tremendously popular on Wall Street. In 1998, they misinterpreted the market outlook and ordered some disastrous wrong moves that caused huge losses to the fund. The situation soon got out of hand, and the fund ended up being rescued by the Federal Reserve to avoid a catastrophic impact on the entire financial system.

These three well-known cases have something in common: They were wrong decisions made by top executives who were the best in their fields at that time. It is clear that their decision-making system did not work properly at all. I could compile an endless list of corporate mistakes, cases that occurred in the last few years, months or recent weeks, even yesterday! These mistakes are part of management history and today mistakes continue to play a key role both in political and corporate life (in Appendix 2, you can find 83 real-life examples).

Errors have become more frequent due to the evolution of the environment. We talked already about VUCA world, a more volatile, uncertain, complex and ambiguous context in which to make decisions. Human nature remains the same (our capabilities are not scalable), management has not changed that much (we keep and use the same basic references as always), but the competition is fiercer every day and the scenario has been dramatically transformed by the technology, the ecology and the evolution of people's needs. Thus the variables affecting any management decision have multiplied by several factors in recent decades.

According to James G. March,[28] "The confusion and complexity surrounding decision-making is underestimated. Many things are happening at once. Views and aims are changing, and so are alliances among those concerned. What has to be done is not clear, nor is how to do it. In this topsy-turvy world, in which people do not comprehend what is going on, decisions may have little to do with the processes that supposedly make them, and organizations do not know what they are doing." It sounds a bit apocalyptic, but it certainly has a point.

We speak of decision-making as a generic concept but the 'complexity factor' affects any area of the organization. In addition, management errors can also occur in any area of the organization. Strategy is more complicated than ever, but Human Resources matters are more difficult, too, as well as sales, customer service, finance, operations, marketing or technology.

In the survey, the errors given by the respondents occurred within the following activities:

General strategy	44
Human resources	13
Sales and customer service	9
Finance and investment	7
Production and operations	6
Marketing and product design	5
Technology	2

I will choose an example from each category to illustrate the types of errors that decision makers tend to have in mind (the number shows the order of the example in Appendix 2):

GENERAL STRATEGY

14 | Trying to expand in a foreign market based exclusively on technical advantages and without considering key factors such as legislation or taxation.

HUMAN RESOURCES

78 | Letting a person stay longer than appropriate in a position by assuming a) he would change b) fear of him being absolutely necessary.

SALES AND CUSTOMER SERVICE

7 | Not being transparent with the customer (in a B2B framework). The customer eventually realized that critical information was not being shared, and the result was a substantial loss of trust.

FINANCE AND INVESTMENT

49 | The decision to postpone the repatriation of dividends from the Brazilian branch based on the high interest paid in the country in 2017–2018. Currency risk assessment was overly optimistic.

PRODUCTION AND OPERATIONS

45 | Error of assessment due to fear of change, which caused the loss of an opportunity derived from the digitization of processes.

MARKETING AND PRODUCT DESIGN

52 | The error consisted in developing a new product line and not deciding on the necessary changes in the organization to create the infrastructure to support the new line.

TECHNOLOGY

12 | The purchase of a software tool that did not work out any problem or add any extra value, although it made the processes far more complicated.

Management errors can be the subject of other different classifications. A typical one would differentiate them into strategic, tactical and operational errors. Strategic mistakes are those related to corporate goals, culture and values, long-term plans, markets-competitors-customers, value proposal, partnerships and alliances, distribution channels and so on. Tactical mistakes would be those affecting the decisions made in the deployment of the strategies along each area or activity of the organization and are usually linked to key performance indicators. Operational mistakes occur when executing a task or mandate and are typically repetitive and/or programmed.

The survey provided us with good examples of two types, strategic and tactical mistakes. Here below is one example of each:

STRATEGIC

75 | Absolute focus on service management without worrying about updating the product portfolio.

TACTICAL

17 | Underquoting on a complex but promising project.

However, I was able to find only one single example of an operational type, something that we could already expect, considering that I was dealing with managers. This was the case:

OPERATIVE

57 | When organizing an event, there was a communication error between the supplier and my department, so all the layout (tents, stages, etc.) had to be changed the day before the start.

In this sense, Simon[29] makes a distinction between two polar types of decisions: programmed and unprogrammed. 'Programmed' decisions can be understood as equivalent to 'operational' ones because they will be executed according to a procedure that has been previously worked out. The decision maker does not need to bring about a new approach each time. Attending a customer request or determining an appropriate salary for a job could be good examples of programmed decisions. Otherwise, decisions are unprogrammed when there is no black-and-white method to address the problem or situation, either because it is nothing that has been experienced before or because of its complexity. These are the decisions that fall on the seat of a manager.

Richard Thaler also hits the nail on the head when he explains why rational – expected utility – theory was doomed to be contested:[30] "The model of human behaviour based on the premise that people optimize is and has always been highly implausible. For one thing, the model does not take into consideration the degree of difficulty of the problem that agents are assumed to be solving." Once again, the 'difficulty/complexity' factor suggests that, when it comes to management decisions, hitherto known behavioural theories could fall short of arguments and would require the managers' input for a more thorough picture.

In the survey, we ask two questions that might help us think a bit further about the types of decisions and mistakes. Question 2 asks: "How would you classify the complexity of the decision made in your example?" and leaves four possible answers:

a) A simple decision in which the cause-effect relationships were well known
b) A difficult decision due to the large number of elements to take into consideration
c) A complex decision with relevant potential influence on several stakeholders
d) A critical decision that could jeopardize the future of the organization

Only 20.9% of the respondents noted that the decision they chose as a management mistake was simple. The survey confirms something we suspected: management decisions are mainly difficult or complex (47.7% of responses) and many may prove critical (31.4% of responses).

The first question of the survey asks: "How would you classify the decision made in your example?" and gives again four possible options:

a) A critical error: it had a relevant effect on the future of the organization
b) A serious error: it had a relevant effect on key performance variables of the organization

c) A controllable error: its consequences could be controlled without large cost or effort

d) A restricted error: it affected just one part of the organization but not the whole

If a respondent is asked about an example, they will tend to give a meaningful one: an error that looks like a good example. This is confirmed by the results: 37 consider their example a critical error, 25 a serious error, 20 a controllable error and only 3 believe their example was a restricted error.

Now, if we take complexity and relevance as classification criteria, we will obtain a characterization of management mistakes as according to the following matrix. We draw a large and dark rhombus when the occurrence in the survey is higher than 15%, a medium rhombus when it is between 10 and 15%, and a small and light rhombus when it is less than 10%:

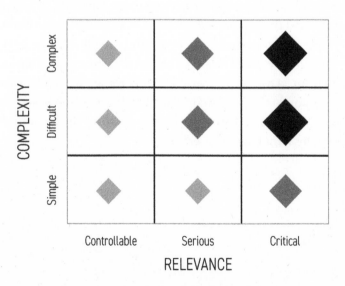

FIGURE 3: RELEVANCE – COMPLEXITY MATRIX

By doing so, we can identify three areas in which to classify management mistakes:

- Highest occurrence: difficult or complex decisions of critical relevance
- Medium occurrence: difficult or complex decisions of serious relevance and simple decisions of critical relevance
- Low occurrence: any decision of controllable relevance and simple decisions of serious relevance

It seems quite clear that the respondents assign a certain degree of complexity to management issues. Furthermore, I would bet that most of them would tend to agree with McCall & Kaplan[31] when they state that "Given this complexity, it is no surprise that the consequences of managerial action are not always clear victories or defeats." Another suggestive classification of management errors could be that which divides them between the generally accepted errors and those about which there is more debate or doubt.

Yes, an error is a relative term, and the blurrier the environment, the more relative the error. Who can determine when an error has occurred? An error in what measure or proportion? Compared to what other option? Based on what objective? It is time to clarify what we should understand by 'a management error.'

3.3 WHAT WE CONSIDER A MANAGEMENT MISTAKE

Let's remember the typical exercise in which one must choose between two options: to play or not to play. So, you have a 50% chance of winning €1,000 and a 50% chance of losing €600: Would you play? A basic calculation will tell us that the 'net value' of playing is positive in €200. So, we should play. But following the aforementioned 'prospect theory,' we know that many will not play. Does this mean they are wrong? We are facing a problem with only two options and clear odds. I mean, there is no complexity or uncertainty, but we are still not 100% sure whether or not 'playing' is the right decision to make. Imagine that losing €600 leaves you without any money. Should you play anyway? You may believe that there will be an upcoming opportunity to play under more advantageous circumstances. In fact, you may have learned about a new opportunity in the near future to play in much better circumstances. In that case, you'd better save your money and wait for the next occasion, right?

Now let's think about real-life decisions:

- Moving to a new office this year: is it a good or a bad choice?
- Replacing the current ERP software?
- Is it wise to sue a long-time provider who does not meet our new requirements?
- Hiring a risk-taking CFO now that business margins are decreasing?
- Should we launch a marketing campaign for an unprofitable segment?
- Could we propose a salary increase to motivate our staff?
- What would be the fair KPIs for that area?
- Shall we go for a smaller product while giving up some capabilities?

We could be adding more and more decisions to be made by managers at any company any time. It does not seem easy to set reliable probabilities of success for these kinds of choices.

The examples above imply a two-choice question: either you do it or you do not. But most of the time, even when it does not seem like it, there are more than two alternatives to decide between. Let's pick the first example, "moving to a new office." As long as we think a bit, we might be able to find a solution other than the obvious 'yes / no' option. Indeed, we have the possibility to stay or move; that seems to be the choice to make. But what if we propose to buy the office we have been renting, or sign a property lease, or change the lease conditions, or carry out a convenient renovation or rent a nearby complementary office? Quite frequently, the two-choice decision may turn into a multiple-choice decision after a thorough analysis of the problem. Furthermore, if we finally move, we can do it immediately or wait a while, move the entire staff or just some of them, and we must decide where to go, which kind of facility we need, what price we should pay, what to do with the former facility, etc. Digging deeper, we discover that an array of alternatives opens up once we thoroughly analyse the problem, and these can still be multiplied when we start the implementation. In fact, the success of the decision will depend mainly on the ability to implement it.

Even when the decision can look simple, it may become complex as new elements are incorporated into the analysis. Assigning probabilities to the various options that arise gets increasingly difficult. Just as it is difficult to determine the chances of success of each option, it is hard to measure the relative outcome of a particular decision. Because, to see if the decision is a good one, it must be compared with each possible option. Moving the headquarters to a new location under certain conditions may have saved 10% of the expenses. All right, so was it a good or a bad decision?

To adequately answer that question, one should know the results that would have been obtained with each of the possible options. In addition, the relocation of the headquarters could have had an impact not only on expenses but also on efficiency, staff motivation, the image of the company, general coordination, etc. How can you include these considerations in your analysis of results? It seems that, in a simple context, you could easily determine whether a decision was good or bad based on its outcome. But in a complex context, the distinction can be really tricky to draw.

Klein states[32] that: "Poor outcomes are different from poor decisions. The best decision possible given the knowledge available can still turn out unhappily ... I define a poor decision ... in the following way: A person will consider a decision to be poor if the knowledge gained would lead to a different decision if a similar situation arose. Simply knowing that the outcome was unfavourable should not matter. Knowing what you failed to consider would matter." This seems an interesting point of view according to which the decision process must be regarded at least as important as the outcome of the decision (at this stage we will speak of 'process,' which is the term used in most studies and decision theories; later in the book we will break down the concept into 'method,' applied to individuals, and 'system,' applied to organizations).

Francesca Gino[33] follows Klein's conclusion when she writes: "The outcome bias is costly to organizations. It causes employees and leaders to be blamed for negative outcomes even when they had good intentions and used a thoughtful decision-making process, considering all the information that should be taken into account." In fact, there is some controversy in management literature about the effects of an 'outcome orientation' versus a 'process orientation': Siegel-Jackson and Yates[34] state that process accountability prompts more accurate judgments and leads to a better decisions, whereas for Bart de Langhe[35] this performance advantage does not extend to more complex decisions.

Gustavo Barros,[36] in his article about Simon's concept of rationality, gives another complementary clue when he writes: "Behaviour is procedurally rational when it is the outcome of appropriate deliberation. Global rationality is understood as substantive in the sense that it is only concerned with what has the choice done, its result. The concept of procedural rationality focuses on how the choice is done. The crucial issue in the distinction between substantive and procedural rationality lies in the proposition that the decision-making process and, therefore, also the agent who carries out this process, influences crucially the decision result. Simon's research in the area of cognitive science demonstrated that, in complex situations, the choice taken and its result strongly depended on the particular process that generated it, and not only on the objectives that oriented it. Hence, it becomes indispensable to know the process by which the choice is taken."

Let's see a fictitious example to analyse the impact of process and outcome in decision-making. *Noname Distribution Co.* has a cash surplus of $2 million. *Noname's* CEO assigns one million to the CFO and the other million to the CPO. The company plans to open a new market operation in 12 months and will need a 10% return on those funds. The financial manager carries out a rigorous analysis of the financial markets, makes some diversified investments according to rational expectations and does some trading on a conservative basis. The procurement manager does nothing with the money until the last month; at that moment he hands out the million to a black-market broker who makes two fortunate transactions and earns a 25% return. A few weeks before the CEO's deadline, a virus spreads worldwide and the value of the CFO's investment drops finally by 15%. Which of the two managers made the right decision?

An adequate process does not guarantee achieving a good outcome and a good outcome does not guarantee having followed a right process. In between the two concepts, something may arise: the influence of uncontrolled and unpredictable factors beyond your reach. Examples of these circumstances could be the lack of performance of a third party or a new element that came out of the blue:

a legal change, an abrupt cost variation, an unforeseeable reaction from a competitor, a failure in the supply chain, an evolution of the market contrary to your interests, the modification of corporate goals, the loss of a basic resource, a fortuitous accident ... the list would be endless.

Simple luck can also be one of those factors. Professor Gosling claimed[37]: "Luck plays a part in success of all kinds. Staying on top takes luck as well as skill. But we often mistake one for the other." Already in the Introduction of his famous book, *Thinking Fast and Slow*, Kahneman states: "Luck plays a large role in every story of success; it is almost always easy to identify a small change in the story that would have turned a remarkable achievement into a mediocre outcome." Michael Wheeler[38] agrees with both statements: "So it is with any decision: the chain of events that brings you to a choice point will be shaped by luck, good or bad."

The Black Swan[39] of Professor Taleb, as an unpredictable event, could be considered an element of luck. "Our world is dominated by the extreme, the unknown, and the very improbable" states the book, giving us an idea of the key role the unpredictable plays in life. COVID-19 could be an example of a black swan, couldn't it? However, the world suffered from SARS and bird flu in 2005, swine flu in 2009, MERS in 2012 and Ebola in 2015. COVID-19 may not have been so unforeseeable after all. Let's imagine that a friend of ours has been working really hard for the past 10 months and finally opens his tour services company ... on February 1, 2020. It does not matter if COVID-19 was or was not a black swan; it would definitively be a case of bad luck for our friend.

So now we have three factors to understand how to distinguish a good decision from a poor one: process, outcome and unpredictable forces. To work out an accurate description on the concept of 'poor decision,' we will use a matrix that combines the three elements. The two axis are established according to the following criteria:

OUTCOME AXIS

Good outcome: the objective was achieved. If the goal in 'Noname case' were set at a 10% return, a good outcome would have been to get at least that profit.

Neutral outcome: the goal was not achieved though the result was not bad for the organization either. In the case: the result would have been positive but not achieved a 10% profit.

Poor outcome: the result was negative for our organization.

PROCESS AXIS

Thorough process: an adequate process is followed and the key elements are taken into consideration. Identifiable with System 2 (see Section 2.2 about 'dual process of reasoning').

Quick process: the decision is taken after a short period of reflection. Identifiable with 'In-between System.'

No process: immediate decision based on pure heuristics. Identifiable with System 1.

Look at the matrix on page 63 to identify the three different areas that will allow us to distinguish between a good and a bad decision:

GOOD DECISIONS AREA

a) If you followed a thorough process and got either a neutral or a positive outcome, you are considered to have made a good decision.

b) If you followed a quick process and got a positive out-come, you are also considered to have made a right decision; your experience was good enough to under-stand the problem and find the adequate solution.

'IT ALL DEPENDS' AREA

a) If you decided with no reflection and the outcome happened to be positive, the decision could be con-sidered right unless the positive results were due to the effect of unpredictable factors.

b) If you followed a quick process and got a neutral out-come, the decision would be considered also neutral unless unpredictable factors had some influence: if there was positive influence, the decision was proba-bly wrong, whereas if it was negative influence, then the decision was probably right after all.

c) If you followed an adequate process but did not get a good outcome, it could be due to a bad decision or a matter of unpredictable factors.

POOR DECISIONS AREA

a) If you made the decision only on the basis of intui-tion and did not get a positive outcome, you are con-sidered to have made a poor decision.

b) If you followed a quick process and got a negative outcome, you are considered to have also made a bad decision; you may have believed that your experience was enough to make the right choice, but it turned out otherwise.

Therefore, a 'Good and Poor Decisions Matrix' would look as follows:

GOOD DECISIONS VS. POOR DECISIONS

		Negative	Neutral	Positive
PROCESS	Thorough	It all depends	GOOD	GOOD
	Quick	POOR	It all depends	GOOD
	None	POOR	POOR	It all depends
		Negative	Neutral	Positive
			OUTCOME	

FIGURE 4: MATRIX TO QUALIFY DECISIONS

In the survey, I included several questions that can help us understand how managers see the distinction between good and bad decisions. Question 6 asks: "As far as the management mistake you described at the beginning of the form, why do you consider it to be a poor decision?" (Multiple choice among nine options.) There was one answer that stood out above all the rest:

g) The decision was inconsistent with the objective pursued

It seems to be a good definition of what a bad decision means. Once put in order, the complete results were as follows:

OPTIONS	RESPONSES	%
The decision was inconsistent with the objective pursued	44	51.2
It was not the best possible option	30	34.9
The decision made the organization lose money	30	34.9
The organization was in a worse position after the decision	29	33.7
Inadequate balance between costs and benefits	27	31.4
The decision was made without the required process of analysis	25	29.1
The decision made the organization assume an important risk	23	26.7
The decision made no sense	10	11.6
The decision focused on the short term and ignored the long-term effects	9	10.5

Let me outline three interesting points of the previous table:
- Thirty respondents show a result-oriented bias versus 25 who show a clear process-oriented approach
- Twenty-nine go for a strategic perspective of reasoning
- Thirty respondents challenge the 'bounded rationality' concept of Herbert Simon (see section 2.2), according to which a good decision may not be the best possible one

In Question 10, I asked the managers a straightforward question: "What do you think can be considered a good decision?," and gave them four options. These were the results:

	OPTIONS	RESPONSES	%
a)	The best option of all the possible alternatives	16	18.6
b)	Any decision which provides a good result to the organization	13	15.1
c)	Any decision made after a thorough process of analysis and consistent with the objective pursued	19	22.1
d)	Both b) and c) look correct to me	38	44.2

According to the previous data, a wide majority of those surveyed favoured a flexible interpretation of what should be considered a 'good decision,' accepting both that which generates a good result and that which follows a strict process of analysis. So, it could be inferred that a bad decision (a mistake, an error) would be the one that either does not follow a complete process or does not obtain a good outcome.

Finally, in Question 13, I gave the managers nine situations, quite similar to those exposed in the 'Good & Poor Decisions Matrix,' and asked whether they considered each one a good decision, a poor decision or if their assessment depended on the circumstances. Only the option a) *A decision made through a solid analytical process that met the required goals* was regarded as a clear good decision. Three others were considered bad decisions, and the opinions were not clear about the other five. These were the conclusions on the answers to Q13:

	OPTIONS	RESPONSES
a)	A decision made through a solid analytical process that met the required goals	Good decision
d)	A decision made after a little reflection that met the required goals	Depends on circumstances with a positive bias
b)	A decision made through a solid analytical process that had got a positive outcome but did not fully meet the required goals	Depends on circumstances with no bias
g)	An automatic or spontaneous decision that nevertheless met its required goals	Depends on circumstances with a negative bias
h)	An automatic or spontaneous decision that got a positive outcome but did not meet the required goals	
e)	A decision made after a little reflection that got a positive outcome but did not fully meet the required goals	Between bad decision and dubious assessment
c)	A decision made through a solid analytical process that did not meet the required goals	Sort of a bad decision
f)	A decision made after a little reflection that did not meet the required goals	Bad decision
i)	An automated or spontaneous decision that did not meet the required goals	

We can conclude that the managers' opinions tend to be stricter than the criteria applied in the 'Good & Poor Decisions Matrix.' Whereas in the matrix three types of decisions would be considered right, according to the managers, only one case would be truly good. Anyhow, the results of the survey do confirm the validity of using three factors (outcome, process and circumstances) to distinguish the good decisions from the bad ones, that is, from management errors.

A final reflection in this section: I have been talking about 'decisions' in general as if the decisions were monolithic and did not depend on the profile and/or situation of the decision maker, which is not accurate, because the evaluation of the 'result' of a same choice may vary depending on who made the decision. In February 2021, the first tweet ever issued was sold in an auction on the platform Valuables for $2.9 million. The tweet had been previously turned into a non-fungible token (NFT), which is a one-of-a-kind digital asset represented on a blockchain. Let's imagine that the purchase was not an impulsive move but a reasoned and well-informed decision. How can you tell if it was foolish or wise? We may not be able to see the final outcome of the decision in the near future, and there will surely be a consensus on how complicated it is to forecast the price evolution of that NFT.

So was it a good or a bad decision after all? There is only one answer to the question: it depends on the goal of who made the decision. If investing in the NFT markets was like plunging into the unknown for the decision maker who, on top of that, only had a few euros/dollars/pounds in the bank, the $2.9 million bid for the first tweet seems pretty crazy. If they had a fortune of, say, $100 million invested in non-volatile assets and want to diversify the investment in search of higher returns, the gamble could make some sense. And if they were a global partner in the arts market and tried to open a 'blue ocean' where investors evaluated the uniqueness of crypto-pieces, then the transaction may even seem smart because it can mark a price benchmark for the next operations.

The above example clarifies the concept of the 'result' or 'outcome' when dealing with the assessment of decisions. The evaluation of the result must be different depending on the goal of the decision maker. And that is why 'objectives' are such a key element in any study of management decisions. Then, finally, we could end with the conclusion that, to evaluate whether a decision was correct or not, it is necessary to take into consideration the decision-making process, the relevant circumstances and the results obtained as understood in relation to the goals previously defined.

3.4 THE RIGHT OR WRONG FOCUS

In September 2019, Thomas Cook collapsed after 178 years in business. Thomas Cook was a huge global travel group, with annual sales of £9 billion, 19 million customers a year and 22,000 staff operating in 16 countries. The group had reported a £1.5 billion loss for the first half of its financial year, with £1.1 billion of the loss caused by the decision to write down the value of My Travel, the business it merged with in 2007. However, the financial report already warned of 'further headwinds' for the rest of the year, Brexit included. The group ended up putting its airline up for sale in an attempt to raise badly needed funds. Later on, the troubled operator announced it hoped to seal a rescue led by China's Fosun, its main stockholder, but the creditor banks issued a last-minute demand so that the travel company needed to find an extra £200 million. On Sunday, 22 September, the situation was as follows:

The hedge fund CQS had walked away from talks to provide urgent liquidity to the ailing travel company; all the possible scenarios that were on the table had been ditched after it became clear that the company could become insolvent within hours. Around 165,000 travellers would have to be flown back to the UK from their holiday destinations. The company needed to secure a £200 million lifeline following a demand from its lenders or face being placed into bankruptcy proceedings in the early hours of Monday. A senior executive of the group approached the government to get the £200 million needed to prevent the crash.

We can figure out the elements that could have been taken into account before making such a crucial decision: the company's customer base, its personnel, structure and resources, its know-how in the industry, the strategy to reactivate the corporation, the potential cost of any solution to taxpayers, financing and logistics of the repatriation of travellers, the alternatives of government participation or the general image of the British tourism sector would be key elements of the analysis. However, at the end of the day, that already iconic figure of £200 million emerged as an essential element, sweeping away all the meaningful factors regardless of the overall consequences of the decision.

Too often numbers acquire a prominence that they do not deserve. Numbers are important when facing a numerical problem. The history of management is full of cases in which the financiers took charge of the situation and so the discussion leaned heavily toward the financial aspects, as these were unquestionable. And that is why I say that some of the decision errors come from not understanding the type of decision that managers face. Before a manager even begins to analyse the information or the nature of the problem to be solved, they must understand the type of decision they must make.

In previous sections, I highlighted the relevance of complexity when studying management decisions. Managers must deal with plenty of elements, with different agents involved, normally with a turbulent context and frequently with the potential reaction of third parties affected. In general, some decisions will be straightforward, some will involve some complexity, and some will reach a peak of maximum complexity. For the sake of reasoning, I will divide the decisions in terms of complexity into two main groups: major and minor.

The other main criterion for classifying decisions will be context. Positive theories developed their body of analysis from a certain context where the information and options were known as well as the probabilities of success of the events. Later theories that amended the positive theory grasped the concept of uncertainty as a critical factor. In real life, it is rare to be able to collect and process all the information available on a problem or topic, and it is equally rare to be able to accurately predict the effects of every action. It is clear to all that different levels of uncertainty have a great influence on the classification of decisions. Again, for the sake of reasoning, we will deal with two categories of context: certain and uncertain.

From the classification of section 3.2 between programmed and unprogrammed decisions, I will consider only the latter type. As an example of this: In March 2021, the Emergent BioSolutions manufacturing plant in East Baltimore made the terrible mistake of mixing up the wrong ingredients for a COVID-19 vaccine and ruined 15 million doses. It was an extremely serious mistake due to an operational issue rather than a managerial decision problem. The chart on the next page contains a meaningful classification of tactical and strategic decisions:

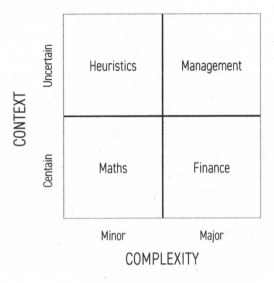

FIGURE 5: MATRIX TO CLASSIFY DECISIONS

Let's start with the bottom layer, the 'certain context.' A bad decision in a certain context is mainly due to a lack of knowledge. If one knows the predictable behaviour of each variable in the decision to be made and how to obtain the result of their interaction, they can obtain the final outcome of each solution. A certain context allows an objective evaluation if the mathematical, statistical or financial tools are properly managed. There will always be room for interpretation or simulation but, in any case, in a given context, the analysis will admit a quantifiable treatment.

A decision maker can solve a minor decision in a certain context through mathematics. Let's imagine purchasing new equipment to strengthen the company's production capacity. There are two possible providers with the same type of contract and guarantees. Vendor A offers a lower price but a longer delivery period and the included installation service; Vendor B offers a higher price but a shorter delivery and no installation. Knowing the production revenue per day and the internal cost of the installation, the manager in charge of the operation could evaluate which offer would be most profitable for the company.

If the decision involves a range of returns, varied risk premiums and different markets, products and terms, then it will require extensive knowledge of financial dynamics. However, eventually the success of the operation will depend on the use of the appropriate tools and the accuracy of the calculation. Even with room to choose between options, in this type of decisions, the numbers are and must be the prominent element of the decision. The scenario can be problematic and really complex, but if the decision maker is an expert, they will finally achieve the goal set. Let's go back to the previous case. The provider in the example allows the equipment to be paid for in a combination of currencies, term charges and hedging products. The decision will be conditioned by yields, rates and risk premiums among other financial variables but, at the end of the day, the best choice will be identifiable. I am not saying that financial products are traded under conditions of certainty; what I am saying is that most complex decisions under conditions of certainty can be solved by financial calculations.

Heuristics dominates the cell where minor relevance and uncertain context intersect. This is a field widely explored by decision theories and where intuition and the mind-set play a key role. Imagine that a team member walks into the manager's office and says, "We would prefer a two-year agreement, but they push for a longer period." The manager proposes straightaway: "Well, offer them a five-year agreement that includes a termination clause applicable after six months based on results." The manager does not need to analyse the situation further. They have already been through similar situations and have accumulated enough experiential knowledge to realize that this solution would be the right one for both parties: heuristics comes into play.

Heuristics is really helpful because it can save managers lots of time and resources. But they can also lead to severe problems if applied to complex decisions. As Bazerman and Moore[40] state, "It may be inevitable that people will adopt some way of simplifying decisions. But reliance on heuristics creates problems, primarily because people are typically unaware that they rely on them. Unfortunately, the misapplication of heuristics to inappropriate situations leads people astray. When managers become aware of the potential adverse impact of using heuristics, they become capable of deciding when and where to use them and, if it is to their advantage, eliminating certain heuristics from their decision-making repertoire."

Finally, we find 'management' in the intersection of 'uncertain context' and 'major complexity.' Applying 'management' to a decision means defining an appropriate objective, setting a number of reasonable alternatives, compiling relevant information and carrying out an adequate analysis to reach a well-argued solution. Let's examine this through an example from our catalogue of management mistakes:

22 | Poor site selection for a retail store.

I knew a case of this. El Ganso, the Madrid men's fashion brand, opened its first store in Germany in June 2014. El Ganso selected Berlin for its first German establishment, specifically at 19 Münzstrasse. The location had been chosen at the suggestion of a local real estate office. Münzstrasse is a sparsely crowded street in Mitte, near Alexander Platz, and some high-end brands such as Karl Lagerfeld and Scotch and Soda were established there at the time. Sales in the store were barely approaching monthly targets. Marketing actions were proposed by the store manager from the beginning due to the low number of people who normally walked down Münzstrasse, but El Ganso owners were unwilling to change their typical low-profile marketing strategy. After a year in which the sales figures failed to take off, the directors of El Ganso decided to replace the store manager. From that point on, sales began to decline noticeably until the store closed soon after.

In the decisions made concerning the store of El Ganso in Berlin, heuristics prevailed over actual management. The previous experiences of the company in Spain, Italy, France and Mexico convinced the directors to follow the same pattern of behaviour in Germany without noticing that it was a completely different market. The rush to continue the international expansion made them pick the first downtown site that met their size and price requirements, and the 'inconsistency avoidance tendency' (a cognitive bias that I shall explain later in this section) prevented them from designing a more-than-necessary marketing strategy for Berlin.

Poor decisions under uncertainty may be caused by a great deal of different reasons. One of those reasons is the incorrect consideration of the type of decision to make.

The set of relationships among the different categories leads to a series of effects such as those shown in the table below:

WHAT IF	EFFECT ON DECISION
'Heuristics' is applied to the 'management-type' decisions	The chances of making the right decision are greatly diminished
'Heuristics' is applied to the 'maths or finance-type' decisions	It's a wrong move. Doing the necessary calculations is the correct thing
'Management' is applied to the 'heuristics-type' decisions	Extra effort to possibly come up with the same solution
'Management' is applied to the 'maths or finance-type' decisions	It is a lousy and time-consuming move. Making the necessary calculations is the correct one
'Maths or finance' is applied to the 'heuristics-type' decisions	It does not make sense
'Maths or finance' is applied to the 'management-type' decisions	It makes sense when used as an element of the analysis but not as the main factor in the decision

THE REASONS MANAGERS ARE SO OFTEN WRONG

Two years after founding the first online foreign exchange trading company in the country, an opportunity to open an office in Asia presented itself. Knowing the person who was to run the office in Asia, a decision was quickly made to open the office without an intensive analysis. The effort never really took off due to the inability of the person as a manager, the distance and the amount of work and focus that was needed in Europe. After a few years, it was decided to shut down the operation.

The above case is example 39 from our management errors list. The text gives some clues about the reasons for the error, which turned out to be a heavy burden on the forex trading company. It is already recognized that the decision (an important one) was made quickly and without the required analysis. I assume that there was no proper market study or risk assessment and not even second thoughts about the role and profile of the person who triggered the operation. Many things could have been done differently. If deep reasoning had been performed, the forex company could have chosen to forego the operation or handle it with a different approach, hence the outcome might have been different as well.

In defining the naturalistic decision-making setting, Klein identified some real-life conditions such as time pressure, lack of experience, inadequate information, the decision maker's profile, ill-defined goals, poorly defined procedures, wicked circumstances, dynamic conditions or objectives, and lack of team coordination. The limited capacity of the human mind to formulate and work out complex problems is the cornerstone of the concept of bounded rationality introduced by Simon. The basis of Kahneman's work were the so-called cognitive biases that seriously restrain people's ability to make the right decisions. Thaler points out the inability of even seasoned professionals to make successful economic and financial predictions.

In his widely known book *Out of the Crisis*,[41] Professor W. Edwards Deming outlined, as part of his management theory, what he considers to be the five 'deadly diseases' that conditions the performance of managers. Here are those five factors below:

1. Lack of constancy of purpose to plan products and services that will have a market and keep the company in business and provide jobs.

2. Emphasis on short-term profits: short-term thinking (just the opposite from constancy of purpose to stay in business) fed by fear of an unfriendly takeover and the push from bankers and owners for dividends.

3. Evaluation of performance, merit rating or annual review.

4. Mobility of management; job hopping.

5. Management by use only of visible figures, with little or no consideration of figures that are unknown or unknowable.

In the following sections, we shall see how some of these elements – lack of constancy of purpose, emphasis on the short term or problems with figures – were confirmed in our study on wrong decisions.

There is a fairly long list of reasons that could explain why managers make mistakes so often. Some reasons will have more impact than others. We'll find out checking the survey results. As we saw in section 2.3, decision theories have not taken managers much into account in their studies. This is why their assessments are difficult to apply directly to management decisions. Complexity and uncertainty combine to make it almost impossible to draw valid conclusions from lab experiments. I have preferred to ask the managers about the main reasons that explain management mistakes according to their own experience. Question 12 of the survey is worded like this:

How important are the following elements for making a good decision?

There are four possible answers:
1. If you think it is not important
2. If you think it is somewhat important
3. If you think it is fairly important
4. If you think it is absolutely critical

To analyse the result, I used a simple index giving each answer its own value (1 point for answer 1, 2 points for answer 2, and so on) and calculated the right proportion for a maximum of 100 points. I preferred to ask the question in a positive mode and understand that those that are most important elements for making a good decision will also be the critical factors for making a mistake.

The results can be grouped into four categories:

A_{Q12} Only one reason above 90 points: the correct definition of the objective

---

B_{Q12} More than 80 points: reasons about the depth of the analysis and the profile of the decision maker

An accurate evaluation of the risks faced by the decision	86.6
The knowledge of the decision maker	84.3
The experience of the decision maker	84.0
Being able to understand the context affecting the decision	83.4
Being able to understand the market and industry trends affecting the decision	83.4

The distinction between short-term and long-term effects	82.6
Being able to take into consideration all the parties affected by the decision	81.1

C_{Q12} Around 70 points or more: mainly team, process and information reasons

The team and advisors of the decision maker	77.6
The availability of an effective information system	75.3
A clear process in the organization to make decisions	74.7
The use of extensive information	73.5
The tendency of the manager to make team decisions	72.7
The availability of enough time to carry out an adequate analysis	72.4
A good financial study	71.8
The leadership style of the decision maker	70.1
The alignment between personal and corporate goals	69.8

D_{Q12} Final category: organizational issues and specific qualities of the decision maker

A clear organization chart and allocation of responsibilities	66.9
The personality of the decision maker	66.0
The level of the operational stress in the organization	63.7
The level of personal conflicts in the organization	60.8
The mood and state of mind of the decision maker	59.6
The professional education of the decision maker	57.6
Good luck	50.9

In Q14, the survey asked:

Going back to the management mistake you described at the beginning of the form, which do you think were the reasons for the mistake?

I tried to confirm, with the reality of the examples given by the managers, the impressions obtained from Q12. Most of them were confirmed, but not all. Below, I sum up the responses to that key question. I followed the same calculation method applied for Q12:

A_{Q14} There are three factors that prevail over the rest and with a considerable difference of relevance between them (over 70 points):

An underestimation of the risks involved	80.2
The profile of the manager who made the decision	76.7
An inadequate consideration of some context elements	71.8

B_{Q14} Reasons with between 60 and 66 points, a set of mixed elements:

To prioritize short-term over long-terms effects	66.0
An adequate analysis process was not followed	65.4
The influence of cognitive biases	63.7
An overvaluation of the organization's capabilities	63.1
A poor selection of the necessary information	60.5

C_{Q14} Reasons with more than 50 points and less than 56, another set of elements with no bond in between (note that the definition of the objective falls into this group):

Not taking into account a possible reaction from customers	55.2
The organization does not have a clear organization chart	52.0
Stress, limited time available	51.2
Ineffective or not clear definition of the objective	50.9

D_{Q14} Reasons that seemingly have less influence on making management mistakes:

Misleading calculations; bad work with numbers	48.8
Not taking into account a possible reaction from competitors	44.5
Lack of a financial study	44.5
Bad luck	35.2

A more in-depth analysis of this data will be shown in the following sections.

4.1 THE RELATIVE IMPORTANCE OF OBJECTIVES

In Q12 of the survey, 61 managers out of 86 agreed that "the correct definition of the objective" is essential to make a good decision, and 19 thought that it is quite important. Therefore, it became the first factor for making correct decisions according to the survey. However, if we look at Q14, "the clear definition of the objective" was only the 12th out of 16 reasons among the real causes of the management errors in our directory. How can this be?

An explanation would be that managers consider the definition of the objective as being the first factor for a good decision, but at the end of the day, the objectives are reasonably well set because they do not prompt too many mistakes. Nevertheless, we find that 14/86 of the managers pointed out that the poor definition of the objective was "one of the main reasons" for the mistake to occur and 15/86 that it had 'a relevant effect.'

It is curious to verify how most of decision studies talk about meeting an objective without considering whether it is well established. What if the bad decision comes precisely from a poor definition of the objective? Error number 51 on our list of management mistakes can help us see the effect of objectives on decisions.

> 51 | A greedy strategy based on rapid expansion and aggressive selling tactics. Hiring managers oblivious to corporate culture and focused on short-term results. Expansion to unknown markets already saturated, assuming high-risk operations with prices lower than those of the competition. Prioritize short-term volume over credit quality. This strategy exacerbated the attitude of the managers whose prestige and compensation depended on how quickly their business areas grew.

I know the case. The company in the example had size as its primary goal. They wanted to be big, to boast to their peers of their capacity for growth. Its CEO was truly proud of himself and his main aspiration was to become a widely admired social leader. The entire organization was imbued with this ambition and all its actions aimed to bring the company to higher positions in the industry rankings. Decisions taken to pursue this essential objective were considered correct; otherwise, decisions that attempted to moderate business growth by adopting a more risk-conscious policy were considered foolish. So most of the decisions were consistent with the goals and the managers were rewarded accordingly, but the company ultimately went bankrupt.

Establishing an objective is a decision in itself and that decision becomes the mandate of another decision maker who is usually lower down in the organizational chart. They must assume that objective and act accordingly. Objectives and decisions make up a continuous chain of actions that determine the dynamics of an organization. Each action influences the next in an ongoing stream of interrelated decisions. So, of course, "the correct definition of the objective" is a critical issue for the success of the company. However, who determines if the first objectives, the ones that will inspire the rest, are well or badly established?

Gary Klein, who already spoke of 'ill-defined goals" in his bestseller *Sources of Power*, highlights[42] the need to question the objectives of the organization especially when addressing 'wicked problems,' that is, complex situations under uncertain contexts (so many in management!). These are Klein's words: "Skilled managers have to be able to adapt and perform trade-offs between different goals and constraints. And then there is the challenge of wicked problems: goals and objectives that cannot be carefully defined in advance. Problems for which there is no 'right' answer. Wicked problems can arise because not enough is known at the outset to specify all features of the goal, or because there is no optimal solution, or because of different stakeholder communities, or because a rapidly changing context is likely to render the original goals irrelevant."

The imaginary company HYQK enters a new market. This is a decision triggered by certain goals. They may want to grow, expand market segments, diversify risks and generate economies of scale. A year later, HYQK may have turned its objectives toward knowing the particular procedures of the distributors of the new market, challenging one of the products of the competition and winning a certain niche that they have found especially promising. A year later, we could find them struggling to optimize the resources allocated to the project, negotiating a business agreement with a local partner, building an online operation and adjusting the image of their products to a younger layer of the population. When HYQK made the decision to enter the new market, it had assumed a theoretical scenario that had little to do with reality once it had settled down. After three years, it had not achieved any of the objectives set at the beginning. Where was the problem:

in the goals themselves, in the strategy outlined to meet the objectives or in the execution of the strategy?

We can now ask ourselves: is it better to set precise and detailed objectives and goals or to leave them vague and imprecise? Let's see a real and meaningful case. It is a multinational company that produces and markets tiles and bathroom fixtures. Not long ago, it started operations with bathroom furniture, but this line of business never took off. They finally made the decision to acquire one of their main furniture suppliers. They were really determined to turn things around right away. A senior company executive was appointed to lead the negotiations with the goal of closing a deal quickly and smoothly. The negotiations focused mainly on the conditions of the acquisition, and after a few months they sealed the operation. Everyone was happy, but the honeymoon was short lived. As soon as they started the integration process, multiple large problems arose. Instead of trying to inaugurate an efficient and productive period for both companies, they were immersed in an endless battle to determine who was responsible for each issue, who developed each part of the process and, in fact, to discuss the very nature of that process. If the acquiring company had set clear goals for each key aspect of the integration rather than just worrying about the deal itself, the transition and subsequent evolution would have been much better.

It is not easy to determine the optimal level of definition of the objectives. As James G. March[43] had already argued in 1962, organizations function as a kind of multipurpose political coalition subject to the diverse interests and goals of all stakeholders involved: "The composition of the firm is not given; it is negotiated. The goals of the firm are not given; they are bargained." That sort of *coalition* includes all kind of stakeholders: staff, colleagues, partners, customers, suppliers, advisors, competitors, government, social groups, lobbyists, etc. Each of them has its own interests and preferences, and they probably have in mind a kind of ideal organization to pursue, their own vision of what it should look like and where it should go. If preferences within the organization are not clear, the right objectives are only discovered as organization moves; establishing the precise goals in advance can be both difficult and inconvenient.

So, on one hand we have this uncertain and complex scenario where it does not seem appropriate to set explicit goals. Gary Klein[44] puts it this way: "If the project or program is sufficiently important, the managers will have to start work even with goals that are somewhat vague. They are more likely to achieve an acceptable outcome if they can modify the goals along the way, making discoveries rather than rigidly clinging to the initial objectives." And on the other hand, we have projects or problems that need clear and detailed objectives to guarantee correct development and resolution. The dilemma leads us to a graph where both realities converge:

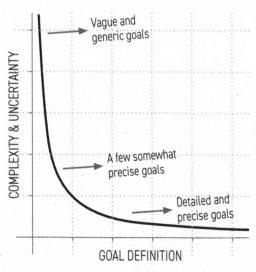

FIGURE 6: GOAL DEFINITION CURVE

As is so often the case, the proper stance for managers would be to take nothing for granted and be flexible enough to adapt their decisions to the evolving position of the organization in the ever-changing scenario that is doomed to compete and survive. I would not say that conclusion comes as a surprise: flexibility is an essential quality for managers that has never been taken into account enough. Of course, objectives are important for making good decisions. But it would be better to establish them according to the type of problem being addressed and the complexity of the scenario in which one is operating. Otherwise, the definition of the objective can become a bad decision in itself and open the door to a chain of management errors.

Finally, the objectives must be clear and shared. It seems obvious, but it is not. Just ask your colleagues and associates what the main goal of the organization or division or unit is, and you will be amazed at the diversity of answers you collect. Ensuring that the people in the organization/division/unit share the same objectives, (I would say the same purpose) should be one of the first duties of a manager.

4.2 THE BALANCE OF RISKS

In October 1952, a self-help book entitled *The Power of Positive Thinking* was published. Written by Methodist pastor Norman Vincent Peale, it was on *The New York Times* bestseller list for 186 weeks, 48 at the top of the nonfiction list. The book, translated into more than 40 languages, sold 5 million copies. Its main message was: as long as you really want something to happen and you strive to make it happen, it will happen. "Believe in yourself!" is how Peale's book begins, and continues with ten rules for "overcoming inadequacy attitudes and learning to practice faith." These are some of the rules:

- Picture yourself succeeding
- Think a positive thought to drown out a negative thought
- Minimize obstacles
- Do not attempt to copy others
- Develop a strong sense of self-respect

Without even knowing it, the attitude of many managers follows the pattern established by Mr. Peale, of whom Donald Trump was one of the most loyal followers.[45] It is supposed that managers must be bold and intrepid, not feel fear before obstacles (risks) and must decide without any hesitation. Often, *the magic wand* is a better appreciated feature than risk valuation; charisma is a more admired quality than thoroughness. In such a scenario, wishful thinking prevails over reasonable thinking, making obstacles and risks invisible. How often does it happen?

Our survey can give us an idea. In Q12, risk assessment, emerges as the third major reason for making good decisions out of 24 possible answers. Forty-seven managers out of 86 claimed that the "accurate evaluation of the risks" is "absolutely critical," and 33 thought that it is "fairly important." Moreover, in Q14, when I asked about the reasons that led to each management mistake of the survey, "An underestimation of the risks involved" came up at the top of the list of 16 factors. In fact, 42/86 respondents think that it was "the main or one of the main reasons" and 24/86 that "it had a relevant effect" on the error. So, unlike the 'objectives,' the consideration of the 'risk' factor over reality reaches an even greater predominance than when the managers responded from a theoretical point of view.

Let's look at one of the examples from the list of management errors. I looked at the list, and I could already pick the first one:

1 | Having opened a whole operation in a new market without any proper analysis, which turned out badly.

I do not know what happened, but I can imagine some of the possible causes of the failure:
- Commercial risks: the customers did not like the company's products, or the distributors did not want to deliver them or the stores did not agree to sell them.

- Operational risks: suppliers not meeting production requirements, a process that never worked properly, a general lack of project efficiency.
- Personnel risks: poorly trained workers, a lack of cooperation from unions or different working conditions than usual.
- Credit risk: difficulties in getting paid.

And it could have also been due to political, environmental, legal or economic risks. There may have been so many risk-linked factors that the decision makers should at least have taken a look at them and made a rough estimate of their probability of occurrence.

Sometimes a manager could reduce the risk they take for their decisions by testing them before full implementation, a not widespread practice. There are several ways to do this. For example, you can investigate the possible reaction of the affected target of a decision. Before moving a price or changing a product, consumers can be consulted to assess how they are likely to take it. A real market test can also be carried out by implementing the decision in a small part of the entire market and only expanding it if the test results are positive. A decision can also be offset by a move in the opposite direction to make it more admissible. You may want to impose tougher conditions on a supplier, for example, and to do so without jeopardizing the relationship you can introduce some advantages on other terms in a new agreement. There are quite a few ways of pre-testing a decision, from a simple previous announcement to a complex market test. Managers can use a wide range of possibilities, each one more or less suitable to each case:

- Pre-announcement: you can test the reaction of your colleagues, clients or opinion leaders before making the final decision.

- Internal test: you can carry out a test or survey among your colleagues and employees.
- Niche test: you can apply your decision to a small group and see what happens.
- A/B testing: you can try two different decisions and compare the results.
- Minimum viable product (MVP): in product strategy, developing an MVP can be an advisable move before incurring a large investment. Provisional solutions based on 3D printing can also be used before developing definitive models.
- Simulation models and games: especially applicable in information technology.
- Trial period: applying the decision during a short period of time and checking the outcome before extending it.

So far in this section, I have been talking about the willingness of decision makers to ignore the risks related to a problem or situation; that is, when they prefer to choose a course of action without taking into account the chances that things might go wrong. At the other end of the rope, we have the decision maker who is unable to make a decision, paralyzed by the fear of taking a certain risk. Cass Sunstein coined the term 'probability neglect'[46] to describe situations in which people focus on the worst-case scenario, which triggers strong emotions and makes them "fail to inquire into the probability that the worst case will occur." They do not act, just in case something terrible happens, even when the chances of it happening are really low. In our list of management mistakes, we find a clear case of it.

40 | Prevented from making an important strategic decision for fear of being wrong.

The example does not provide any additional information, but the very mention of it confirms the effect of fear on taking risks, in the above example apparently due to personal insecurity. I remember a similar case. Our bank was part of a conglomerate that had been formed to finance one of the large projects that was being developed in the country around new mobile telecommunications. A small down payment was made to begin building a basic administrative structure. After a few months, each company involved in the project had to pay most of its contribution. The CEO asked for a final thought. It was then that the investment manager put on the table a 'study' trying to show that if the mobile project failed, it could wipe out the bank's earnings for a whole year. And with little more discussion, the project was abandoned, and we missed one of the best investment opportunities of these decades.

Managing risk in decision-making means identifying what can go wrong, estimating the chances of it happening, assessing the potential effects should each risk become real, and outlining possible solutions to reduce or avoid them. There are two distinct phases: one is to learn about the potential risks and the other to adopt an attitude toward them. The combination of both phases creates eight different situations that define the relationship between decision and risk.

a) Level of learning about risks: Not even thinking about them/knowing the risks and ignoring them/analysing how to deal with them

b) Attitude toward risks: Risk averse/risk neutral/risk taker

POSIBLE EFFECT ON DECISION

Not think about it	Reluctance to decide	Heuristics applied	Reckless decision
Know the risks and ignore them	*Illogical option*	Go ahead trusting own abilities	Risky in big decisions
Analyse a way of dealing with them	Conservative decision	Reasonable decision	Willingness to handle the risks
	Risk averse	Risk neutral	Risk taker

FIGURE 7: DECISION-RISK MATRIX

Therefore, a 'risk-averse' decision maker may be reluctant to decide if they are not able to think about the risks behind a decision and will tend to make conservative decisions when studying the possible risks and estimating their impact on the situation.

A 'risk-neutral' decision maker will apply heuristics when necessary, thus tending not to think about risks in those possibly easy decisions. If the neutral decision maker ignores the identified risks, they may think that the risks will not be so severe that they cannot handle them. Finally, the risk-neutral decision maker will be in the best position to make a reasonable decision when able to analyse a way of dealing with the risks identified.

A 'risk-taker' decision maker will quite possibly select an undesirable option if they do not even think about the possible risks to face and will also tend to make a risky decision if they ignore the identified risks, especially in important situations. And they will be willing to take the risks once evaluated, because they understand that the *bet* is worth it.

There can be no doubt about the close relationship between decision and risk. It seems that the right stance will normally be, as so often in life and in business, at the point of balance.

4.3 THE DECISION MAKER'S PROFILE

In the list of mistakes of the survey, 13 responses were included in the box of human resources. It is the second most important group after general management. Most of the 13 cases had something to do with the profile of the decision maker. Here we have some examples:

5	Hiring a sales manager with the wrong capabilities.
27	The president of a multinational corporation hires a highly qualified CEO without anticipating that his psychological profile would lead him to dispute the chair of the board. The president ended up firing him with the consequent compensation and reputational damage.
34	Deceiving and convincing myself that I could get along with the manager who hired me when I already knew he was very difficult to deal with.
38	Third-generation family members placed in management positions despite inadequate preparation instead of employees with long history and experience in the company.

42	Appointing a person as manager of an area about which they don't even know the basics.
47	Leave the management of the development department in the hands of a technical partner, without specific knowledge for it.
55	A new CEO brought outdated ideas to the company. He decided to weaken our online operations and strengthen traditional channels. Today we are still trying to rebuild what he dismantled some years ago.
73	Ongoing assignation of difficult tasks to people without the proper qualification and experience.

It should not be a surprise. A decision is a personal matter. One can receive reports, studies, news, opinions, advice ... but at the end of the day, you must make a move that will also be influenced by your background, knowledge, experience and capabilities. Not everyone is equally prepared to understand the same kinds of issues. Nor are all equally prepared to occupy the same level of responsibility.

Each kind of job requires a given professional profile that maximizes performance. There will be some profiles with which a manager could do a fair job. But there will also be some others that will be doomed from the appointment. Errors in business decision-making can be due to a wrong fit between each executive and the position they occupy in the organization. A very basic example: if you are extremely shy, a sales position will not suit you. When a person does not have the skills that the job demands, their behaviour as a manager becomes unpredictable. On top of that, cognitive biases are likely to emerge stronger than ever.

I echo the conclusions of Michael D. Watkins to argue that, in a professional career, there are two leaps that typically result in a relevant change of profile: from assistant to manager and from manager to top executive. In his paper *How Managers Become Leader's*[47] Professor Watkins sets seven critical differences in the abilities required to perform successfully as a middle manager and as a senior executive. These are the consequences of this role change on the job profile:

FROM	TO
Specialist	Generalist
Analyst	Integrator
Tactician	Strategist
Bricklayer	Architect
Problem solver	Agenda setter
Warrior	Diplomat
Supporting cast member	Lead role

It is not easy to make the change. Gary Klein, in his previously referenced book, *Streetlights and Shadows*, says: "Lower-level managers are usually given straightforward projects with clearly defined goals, but as they move to positions of greater authority, they are more likely to have to wrestle with wicked problems. Unfortunately, their previous success in tenaciously pursuing the initial goals may now get in their way because wicked problems demand that we revise, not our plans and tasks, but the goals themselves. Research has shown that most mid-level managers cling to their original goals even after it is clear to them that those goals are obsolete."

It seems that flexibility becomes once again the star of all abilities, and it is not so common to find. The divergence in the requirements of different jobs may be behind the Peter Principle,[48] the popular theory of the 1970s. According to this, an employee will be promoted based on their satisfactory performance until they reach a position in which they are no longer competent, as skills required in the previous job are usually different from those of the new one. Thus, companies could be managed by a regiment of executives located on their level of incompetence. They may be making wrong decisions all the time. We should never forget the Peter Principle.

In the survey I conducted, some questions about the profile of decision makers were included. In Q12, I asked about the important elements to make a good decision. Among them, I included some factors related to the managers' profile that obtained the following results (position out of 24 elements):

POSITION	ELEMENT	SCORE
3	The knowledge of the decision maker	84.3
4	The experience of the decision maker	84.0
16	The leadership style of the decision maker	70.1
19	The personality of the decision maker	66.0
22	The mood and state of mind of the decision maker	59.6
23	The professional education of the decision maker	57.6

Note that knowledge and experience rank near the top, while factors like personality, mood and education fall far behind.

There is an additional factor that qualifies the profile of managers: their tendency to make team decisions. Managers rank this element 13 out of 24 as the most important for making good decisions; 44% consider it "quite important" and 24% "absolutely critical." Furthermore, 51% of those surveyed consider that "the team and advisers of the decision maker" are "quite important" and 30% of them "absolutely critical." In Chapter 5 I shall discuss team participation in decisions more fully.

In Q14, the survey asks for the reasons that led to the management error that each respondent gave as an example. This is where the 'decision maker's profile' factor rises to the second position out of a total of 16 elements, leaving no room for doubt about what managers think. Thirty-eight out of 86 thought "the profile of the manager who made the decision" was "the main or one of the main reasons" for the mistake, and 26 thought "it had a relevant effect." Therefore, we better pay attention to this factor if we want to understand the nature of management errors.

Let's rescue for a moment some of the learnings from Chapter 2 to dig deeper into it. Everybody knows managers who tend to make their decisions impulsively; others who decide after a brief reflection and another kind who devote the required time to analysis. Each group defines a different profile of decision maker. In the words of Jonathan Gosling,[49] "They know how to execute, but they are not so adept at stepping back to reflect on their situations. Others face the opposite predicament: they get so mired in thinking about their problems that they can't get things done fast enough." According to Chugh,[50] due to time pressures, most of managers tend to rely mainly on heuristics. The most effective profile would be a flexible one capable of adapting their attitude to the level of complexity of each decision, while always remembering that, as Professor Bazerman stated in his previously referenced book, *Judgment in Managerial Decision-making*, "System 2 logic should preferably influence our most important decisions." By combining the two criteria – decision style and personality as a decision maker – we create a matrix of four profiles that can help us understand the ways in which managers tend to approach decisions:

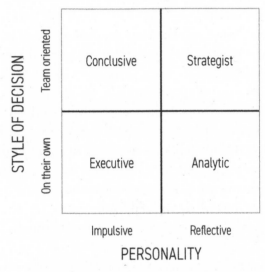

FIGURE 8: MATRIX OF DECISION MAKER PROFILE

a) Conclusive profile: they do not request extensive information to analyse the situation but rather the opinion and point of view of collaborators and advisers. They tend to rush to a conclusion accepted by the team and make the decision accordingly.

b) Strategist profile: they tend to carry out studies and plans that contemplate all aspects of an issue and encourage in-depth analysis and exchange of opinions. They seek consensus in decision-making and that everyone feels that they have been part of the process.

c) Executive profile: they do not shy away from the decision and usually make it quickly on the basis of little information and without hardly consulting anyone. The first impression is what counts. So they are heavily users of the heuristics shortcuts,[51] according to which the decisions are based on previous associations these decision makers keep in their minds.

d) Analytic profile: They want to see all the data and gather as much information as possible before making their choice. They analyse thoroughly and make the decision.

You could tend to think that one profile is better than another. Rather, each type of decision requires a different approach from the decision maker. And each manager profile is better suited to some decisions than others. Again, a flexible profile emerges as the most convenient in any case: Being able to realize what type of decision we are facing and adapt the way of approaching it to make a good choice.

In the survey, only 32 respondents out of 86 (37.2%) believe that "managers adapt their way of deciding to the complexity of the problem to be solved."

4.4 CONTEXT AND COUNTERPARTS

Mateo Salvini is a far-right Italian politician who held the post of Deputy Prime Minister of Italy and Minister of the Interior from June 2018 to September 2019. As Federal Secretary of the Northern League, he was considered one of the main leaders of the populist movement rising in Europe, which is guided by a rightist ideology, oppose immigration and defend economic protectionism.

Il Capitano (The Captain), as he is nicknamed, came into the government after having reached an alliance with *Movimento 5 Stelle* (5 Stars Movement), an eclectic party that was originally left wing although also Eurosceptic and anti-immigration. Despite Luigi Conti, *M5S*'s leader, being appointed prime minister, Salvini placed himself in a dominant role before citizens and the media.

According to most of the polls for the next general election, *Lega* (The North League) was in the lead ahead of the other two prominent parties, *M5S* and PD (Democratic Party). This pushed Salvini to announce a motion of censure against his partner in the government, Prime Minister Conte. He expected Sergio Mattarella, the president of the Republic, to call for new elections after which *Il Capitano* would become prime minister. Those were his plans.

However, after the motion of no confidence, *M5S* and PD negotiated the formation of a new government, and Salvini's League fell from power. As a result, Salvini ceased to be a minister, his party began to fall in the polls and, once he lost his immunity from prosecution, he would face some possible prosecutions for previous issues. It looks like Salvini's decision of tabling a motion of censure turned out to be a serious mistake, probably caused by some misjudgements and because he undervalued the reaction of his opponents and the chance of a new alliance that expelled him from the government. To put it in a nutshell, he misread the context and did not foresee the possible response from the counterparts.

The results of the survey make very clear the weight of contextual aspects in decisions. In the answers to Q12, we find contextual factors in top positions, as we can see below:

POSITION	ELEMENT	SCORE
5	Being able to understand the context affecting the decision	83.4
6	Being able to understand the market and industry trends affecting the decision	83.4
8	Being able to take into consideration all the parties affected by the decision	81.1

Looking at the numbers in detail, 38 out of 86 managers consider "understanding the context" absolutely critical for making a good decision, and 40 fairly important. But it is again in Q14, when asking about the reasons for each management error, where we find that there is no room for doubt. "An inadequate consideration of some elements of the context" ranks third out of 16 causes, with more than 50% of managers stating that this element had a significant influence on the mistake being made.

Knowing PESTEL analysis,[52] it is quite obvious that talking about 'context' refers to political, economic, social, technological, environmental and legal issues. We will not be tempted to dedicate time and space to each aspect, because that is not the purpose of this book. Before making any management decision, one must have a clear understanding of how politics can affect it, what phase the economic cycle is in, what are the main social trends, what impact technological advances may have, the potential influence of care for the environment and the legal conditions to be observed. Disregarding any of these aspects could doom our decision to failure.

In the list of management errors in Appendix 2, there are some examples in which the context contributed to the decision error, for example:

| 11 | The expansion of a branch network of a bank in the hottest moment of the economic cycle. |

Beyond the considerations derived from the typical PESTEL analysis, the context also implies the counterparts that can feel affected. When you play chess, you not only focus on your game but also on your opponent's options. If you attend the training sessions of a basketball team and listen to the statements and harangues of their coach, you will become convinced that they will win. However, as soon as the game begins, you are surprised to find that the opposing team is not only more talented but also better prepared. The success of many decisions will depend not only on the intelligence applied to their analysis but also on the possible reaction of third parties.

In April 2021, 12 football clubs announced the creation of the European Super League. They were six English (Manchester United, Manchester City, Liverpool, Chelsea, Tottenham and Arsenal), three Italian (Juventus, Milan and Inter) and three Spanish (Barcelona, Real Madrid and Atlético de Madrid) clubs. The purpose of the Super League was to ensure that there were official matches between the best European teams every year, which would entail a notable increase in box office collection and, above all, in the television rights of those teams at the cost of blurring national competitions and reducing the income of excluded clubs.

The prospects for the 12 teams were excellent, and they felt they were changing football competition forever. However, they did not count on the reaction of other parties involved. The excluded clubs made their voices heard. Some footballers were outspoken against the project. The British government showed their strong opposition. And above all, the fans took to the streets to shout their anger and shame. The day after the announcement of the start of the competition, the six English clubs left the ship. Soon other clubs joined them. JP Morgan, which was in charge of the financials, issued a statement admitting their error, apologizing for taking part in the project and withdrew. In less than 24 hours, the big operation that was going to prompt a sweeping change in football competition collapsed.

What could those counterparts to which I have been referring in this section be? I would highlight these five groups as the main ones.

1. Customers: I consciously place the client first. Further away or closer to the scope of the decision, customers, as a critical part of the context and ultimate recipients of products and services, are frequently affected by decisions made within the organization, sometimes positively, sometimes otherwise.

2. Competitors: The companies of your industry are alert of your moves and, if they believe your decisions can affect their competitive position, they are likely to make a move on their own as well that may influence the outcome of the original decision.

3. Value chain partners: Some decisions may have an effect on participants in your value chain such as input providers, logistic partners and distributors; also on some outsourced services in production, administration, technology, finance or marketing, for instance.

4. Workmates: Your decisions – and the way you communicate them – may also influence your relationships with colleagues and associates and may cause a reaction if they affect working conditions, the level of motivation of employees or the competences of other units.

5. Administration: The decisions affecting public authorities will not be the most frequent you make, but they may be important if they have something to do with mandatory rules and procedures.

The prisoner's dilemma may be the best-known example of how dependent one can become on the actions of others. In the prisoner's dilemma, you cannot know the outcome of your decision until the other prisoner makes their own move. This is a specific case of game theory. Game theory is a body of mathematical developments formulated to find the optimal decisions to make in different competitive scenarios. Although it is a fascinating field of knowledge, I have not met a single manager who uses game theory when making decisions. However, I have known quite a few cases in which a decision turned out to be a flop because it did not take into account the possible reactions of the third parties involved or the evolution of key elements of the context.

4.5 INFORMATION VERSUS KNOWLEDGE

Imagine your boss asks you to evaluate the purchase of a painting they saw last weekend and thought would be suitable for the meeting room. So you call the gallery and ask for the price of the painting, which turns out to be 50,000 euros (or dollars, or pounds or Swiss francs ...). The company enjoys a comfortable cash position, and the operation does not seem like a great deal after all. The gallerist strongly recommends the purchase based on the supposed high potential of the artist. You do not know much about painters and need to learn about that market. Therefore, you start to study how it works, how prices are determined, what the trends are, who the best-valued painters are, etc. Next, you take a look at the background of the artist your boss is interested in, the main exhibitions they've participated in, who are the top painters with equivalent merit, the price of their works, etc. Finally, you prepare a 35-page report and add several documents as annexes as well as a catalogue of comparable works, some graphics with current prices and a ranking of painters of a similar age to that of the artist. Your conclusion is that there could be other artists at a better cost – potential benefit ratio. Your boss sees all this and congratulates you on such a rigorous job, though it is too late. He had already called a specialist advisor who explained that the uncertainty made any forecast too risky, and that the purchase would be a good option if made without the intention of obtaining a quick profit.

There is a huge gap between information and knowledge that is not easy to fill. Sometimes information certainly means knowledge. If you are a HORECA supplier and read in a local newspaper that Starbucks has decided to enter your market, you will immediately acquire knowledge about what is going to happen because you already know how Starbucks acts when it enters a new market. But if you hear that the new Coldcoffee brand is going to open operations in your market, you have no idea what effect it can prompt on your industry because you do not know Coldcoffee. Therefore, you need more information if you want to gain insight into what is likely to occur as a result of that.

When reflecting before making a decision, you must consider the learning value chain: first you have an objective, then you try to collect meaningful data, you work on turning this into information, you analyse it to arrive at certain knowledge, and you put it into practice to achieve the wisdom. The path is quite demanding, and you will not always be able to make a decision based on 'wisdom,' but you should aspire to do so on knowledge rather than information. The problem is that there is not any evidence[53] that the more information available you have, the broader the knowledge and the better the decision.

I recall this guy who was not the brightest executive of the firm. The CEO had asked him to study the sport harbours industry emerging at that time to decide whether it would be smart to invest in it. He called me one day to show me the two-metre shelves full of reports and books. He had been collecting information about sport harbours from specialized sources and was proud to have put together such an overwhelming *biblioteque*. The problem was that he did not have a clue about what to do with it.

In the introduction of this chapter, I mentioned the work of Professor Edwards Deming. He changed the Japanese economy based on his theories, so I think he has earned the right to be heard and taken into account. Mr. Deming believed that the foundation of good management is what he called 'profound knowledge,' a holistic theory based on optimizing the entire system rather than acting on its individual components. In his theory, Professor Deming established ways of achieving knowledge without reference to information, as if they were independent concepts.

Some people may still rely on the popular phrase "Information is power," but I prefer Sir Francis Bacon's sentence: "Knowledge is power (*scientia potestas est*)." Putting these two phrases together, we realize that the key of the issue is how to turn information into knowledge. This represents a critical challenge for managers and organizations. I will go deeper into this in Chapter 7.

We have a perfect example in the list of management errors of this transcendent difference between information and knowledge:

2	Failing to cover the necessary knowledge about the subject before evicting a settlement of some ethnic minority people.

That was an example given by a councillor from a medium-sized city. She had all the information about the area, the people who lived there, how they had reached that situation, how big the eviction budget was, what the required procedures were, etc. But they had no knowledge at the time of the social dynamics operating in the community, their position before the eviction, and how far they could go in defending their positions. Perhaps managers had some cases like this in mind when they answered the survey I proposed because they placed "The use of extensive information" in position 12 out of 24 elements required for making a good decision, at a slightly lower level than the "team and advisors" or the "process in the organization to make decisions."

In Q14, managers ranked "A poor selection of the necessary information" eighth out of 16 reasons that could cause the management mistake they gave as an example in the survey. In this 'multiple answer' question, 14 managers out of 86 pointed out the information factor as one of the main reasons behind the error, and 26 estimated it had a relevant effect. To be honest, I was expecting higher numbers.

Mikael Krogerus and Roman Tschappeler argue in a TED talk[54] that too little or too much information causes the same confusion in decision makers, which can lead to mistakes. Their reasoning is: "The more we know about any given topic, the more confident we feel to make a decision about it. But there is a tipping point, you can actually know too much ... It's the moment when you start questioning your own knowledge ... And you feel unable to make a decision."

The talk by Krogerus and Tschappeler puts two different problems on the same level: having too little information and having too much information. However, Professor Kahneman qualifies that important conclusion. When explaining the WYSIATI tendency that we shall see in section 4.10, he warns that "The amount and quality of the data on which the story is based are largely irrelevant ... It is the consistency of the information that matters for a good story, not its completeness." As long as the information is coherent, we can feel happy whether it is sufficient or not.

The critical question will then be: how much relevant information does a decision require? The optimal point of information will be that which improves our position before the decision compared to the position in which heuristics places us. We need information to obtain the knowledge that increases the chances of getting it right. And we need information that lessens the potential impact of the main reasons that drive us to make an error (those that we are analysing in the book).

I have been talking about information as an abstract concept that should guide us toward knowledge. The question now is what type of information managers must handle to make sound decisions. I could spotlight here the main content on information and decision support systems spread over thousands of books and papers on the subject. I prefer to emphasize the requirements of the information strategy that any company must follow to ease the decision-making process in the organization. I would use the table below for a better understanding. I have built it from two axes: on the X axis, I put the scope of the information that can be external or internal; on the Y axis, I distinguish if the information should be permanent or ad-hoc.

FIGURE 9: MATRIX OF INFORMATION MANAGEMENT

In Q14 of the survey, "An overvaluation of the organization's capabilities" was identified as the seventh factor causing a management decision error out of 16. This means that an excess of ambition in terms of own resources and capabilities is a fairly common position on the part of managers. The information systems must collaborate to minimize that effect by recording the true situation of the organization structure and assessing how far the company can go from that. In box 1, as permanently available, I include the internal information about the organization that must be an essential part of any decision support system.

In box 1, we also find customers. In organizations there never is a "customer division or department" that is in charge of knowing the customer needs and desires and understanding what they expect in each stage of their relationship with the company. If there is one, it should define what information about customers must be included in any decision support system. The CIO has to be aware of this and fill the possible gap that exists in this regard in the information platform under their responsibility.

In box 2, I also include permanent, systematic information about context and competitors. Here, one must find meaningful information on the evolution and trends of the industry, the markets and the consumers, as well as at least, basic economic information that gives us an idea about the reasonable prospects for the coming years. This set of information will bring us closer to the knowledge of the possible interrelation between context and decision.

In boxes 3 and 4, I include the information you will need to gain the specific knowledge required for a specific decision. Both can be internal on any aspect of your organization and external on any possible aspect that affects the case. No systematization is possible here, but there are at least two issues to take into account: first, the system must be prepared to provide the foreseeable ad-hoc information that the organization's managers may request more frequently and, second, the more specific the requirement of information, the more efficient its application will be. The typical "bring me all the information about ... " requirement is one of the examples of extreme inefficiency that an organization tends to hatch.

Managers need information to gain knowledge. The use of information shows a path of two directions. More often, they face a problem and try to gather information to help them gain the knowledge to make the right decision. Sometimes it can be the other way around: managers receive a piece of information that they understand significant enough to open a process that will lead them to make a certain decision. In these cases, the information gives them the knowledge of a real situation that can become a threat that must be prevented or an opportunity that must be seized, a trigger point from which a seasoned manager must take action. A drop in market share, a decline in margins, the emergence of a new trend, changes in the characteristics of a segment, a worsening of the staff climate, etc. A manager will detect this through their decision support system and will be compelled to act.

A final reflection on the information versus knowledge topic. Sometimes a manager can take a shortcut and gain knowledge without resorting to information gathering. Knowledge collaboration platforms are booming because access to a knowledge network or bank is really worth it. There are many cases that demonstrate the power of knowledge collaboration. Let me bring here a case that I have close to home. The company Empathy Tool turns emerging technologies into platforms for interaction between brands and their audiences using analogic and digital systems that connect the brands' physical and digital spaces. They create innovative experiences based primarily on brain sensing, artificial intelligence, generative content, smart objects and robotics. They have developed projects around the world (United Kingdom, United States, France, Spain, China, Germany, Uruguay and United Arab Emirates) for corporations such as VISA, Hilton Hotels, Renault, Huawei, Tag Heuer, Smirnoff, ADNOC and Estrella de Galicia. All of this was carried out by the two founders, an architect and a journalist, with no prior technological background. They do not have any formal information support system in place. Their secret weapon has been, and still is, knowledge sharing.

4.6 THE LONG-TERM PERSPECTIVE

You may have heard about the '10-10-10' formula[55] engineered by Suzy Welch. Though primarily conceived for personal decisions, its philosophy could also be applied to the business realm. In addition to being easy and effective to implement, it conveys a necessary message. Before any big decision, the 10-10-10 rule suggests not rushing (*watch out for heuristics*) and asking oneself these three questions:

- How will you feel about the consequences of your decision 10 minutes from now?
- How will you feel about it in 10 months?
- How will you feel about it in 10 years?

Suzy Welch's method allows us to put some distance from the hot moment of the decision, relativize the emotional influence and think beyond any immediate effect. In other words, it forces the long-term perspective into the decision. By applying the 10-10-10 rule, one does not lose sight of the strategic objectives of the organization (10 months) and its mission and vision (10 years).

We can find a good example of this aspect in the list of management mistakes. Let me refer to it here:

> 46 | Lack of long-term vision when we ran out of projects and clients, and we did not seek new market niches. That would require collaboration between two departments, which was considered a nuisance. This decision mistake caused a department to go from 10 to three members in one year.

We can also remember one of the examples I gave at the beginning of section 3.2. After the 'Pepsi Challenge' campaign, Coke experienced a drastic drop in demand, so Coca-Cola decided to change its formula to align it with Pepsi's taste. It seemed like a visceral decision and involved a break with the vision of the corporation and a lack of loyalty to its essence and values. They wanted to get the sales figures back ASAP and ignored the effects beyond that. Fortunately for them, consumer protests convinced Coca-Cola's board of directors to cancel the measure, Coke kept its original formula and soon returned to previous consumption figures.

A closer example might be the mobile gaming company that was not making the initially expected revenue from its memory game. The number of players was growing considerably, but the income/player ratio was low. The owners decided to noticeably increase the difficulty of the game as well as the advertising inserts. Revenue increased at the expense of losing players rapidly. For some time they managed to maintain the level of income, but the game lost its momentum and its life cycle was severely shortened. It could have been a long-selling game, but the rush to make a profit doomed it.

I will give you a third example. This was a bakery company that decided to grow by acquiring land to plant wheat. They gathered more than 1,200 hectares and harvested more than 4,000 tons of wheat. They had just bought more land when sunflower prices rose sharply due to extreme weather conditions and the decision of Asian countries to restrict their exports. So, the executives of the company were tempted to diversify the crops and start planting sunflowers. Imagine the many factors that could affect the outcome of the decision: soil health, moisture, depth and composition; effect of temperature, rainfall, wind and other weather conditions; characteristics, requirements and yields of the different varieties; seeds available; need for irrigation; risk of microorganisms, toxicity and pests; minimum efficient extension; complementary crops for intercropping or rotation; technical planting and harvesting equipment; waste treatment; and logistics, packaging, distribution and transformation alternatives, among others. By the time they could have the crops ready, market conditions would have corrected, and the big opportunity would be gone. The case shows how complexity is another important element to encourage long-term thinking and decision-making instead of adopting a short-term decision-making scope.

In his aforementioned book *Out of the Crisis*, Professor Deming highlights the long-term perspective as one of the main keys to making good decisions. He left a 14-point theory for companies to "stay in business and protect investors and jobs." Before proposing the 14 points, he recommends that managers "face seriously the following questions:
- Where do you hope to be five years from now?
- How may you reach this goal? By what method?"

By way of a preamble, he makes it explicit: "Short-term profits are not a reliable indicator of performance of management" and gives suggestive advice: "People who depend on dividends to live on should be concerned, not merely with the size of the dividend today, but also with the question of whether there will be dividends three years from now, five years from now, ten years from now." In fact, let's remember that the second *disease* affecting management that Edwards Deming pointed out was precisely "emphasis on short-term profits." Consistent with these items, the first point on his list is: "Create constancy of purpose toward improvement of product and service;" *constancy of purpose* stands out as the important expression here. "Lack of constancy of purpose" was also the first *disease* identified by Professor Deming leading to mismanagement.

I have to be honest once again and say that I did not expect managers to place such a high premium on the long-term perspective factor. In Q12, 38 out of 86 considered "The distinction between short-term and long-term effects" absolutely critical to making a good decision and 37 that it was fairly important. So, the long-term perspective was ranked seventh among the 24 elements to choose from.

In Q14, 30 managers out of 86 responded that "To prioritize short-term over long-term effects" was one of the main reasons to explain the mistake they offered as an example, and 21 that it had a relevant impact. These numbers placed the long-term perspective as the fourth item among the 16 that could have caused a management error only behind risk, profile and context, the three *star factors* on the list.

The opinion of the respondents confirms something inherent in the manager's role: they must make their decisions by evaluating the permanent effect on the main corporate variables and their position within the market and the community, therefore beyond the impact on their annual bonuses and other secondary or immediate effects. To think long-term, a manager must prioritize a neutral analysis that takes into account the main market trends, the organization's competitive position, its mission and vision, as well as the other complex elements that we are reviewing in this book. Of course, decisions made with that guidance may be more difficult to propose and support, because they may meet some resistance from executives focused on immediate results; I think that predictable fight goes with the salary.

4.7 THE PROCESS (OR THE METHOD)

In section 3.3, I gave details about the close relationship between decision and process. I will not repeat those considerations. What I will do now is examine the opinions of the managers on the relevance of the process for making a good decision. First, we must check question 12 to find the factors linked to the process. There are two:

- The availability of an effective information system
- A clear process in the organization to make decisions

I believe that any organization that makes an effort and dedicates resources to build an information system does so to improve its decision-making process. That is why I included that factor in this section; it is ranked 10th out of the 24 elements necessary to make a good decision. Twenty-two executives (25.6%) claimed that an effective information system is absolutely essential for making good decisions, while 44, just twice as much, think that this element is fairly important.

The 'process factor' itself is one position below the 'information system' and is located in the middle of the ranking, position 12 out of 24. Twenty-six managers believe that a clear process is essential to make good decisions and 36 think it is quite important. That is, they consider it something to take into account, but not one of the most critical elements.

If we go to Question 14, we find that "An adequate analysis process was not followed" factor reaches fifth position among the reasons that caused the management mistakes of our list. It seems like a pretty high place to me. Twenty-four out of 86 respondents believed that the lack of an adequate process was one of the main reasons for the error and 25 thought it was fairly important.

I do not think we should consider a process here as a rigid sequence of ordered tasks to be completed by a specific person. That would be something more appropriate for operations, and we are talking about management. The process should be understood as a dynamic that allows the decision maker to take into account all the key elements and ensure that the point of view of the people with something to say is considered before making the decision. It is time to recall a phrase by Gary Klein already included in section 3.3: "Simply knowing that the outcome was unfavourable should not matter. Knowing what you failed to consider would matter."

We could cite hundreds of articles on the decision process, which I will not do. I will only choose one as an illustration because I found it interesting. First, since it introduces the concept of 'criterion' to which we will appeal later in the book, and second, it also includes a means of synthesizing the analysis and reinforcing the neutrality of the conclusion. The following process was proposed by George E. Monahan[56] and it is laid out in eight steps:

- Read the problem *carefully!*
- Ask yourself what you would like to know

- What is the criterion that will be used to judge whether one set of actions or decisions is better than another?
- Identify conditions and/or restrictions that any plan or action must satisfy
- Define mathematical variables whose values satisfy the previous conditions, restrictions and criterion
- Write the objective criterion in terms of the decision variables
- Express all the restrictions in terms of the decision variables
- Summarize the work

Instead of insisting on theoretical processes, I rather emphasize the idea that a manager does not normally follow a sequenced process but a personal method, conscious or unconscious, to make decisions. This method should include four essential requirements to ensure that we do not overlook ("fail to consider," according to Klein's words) any critical aspect. These are the requirements:

1. Understanding the problem and defining the objective/objectives
2. Assessing or acquiring the sufficient knowledge to make a right decision
3. Identifying the alternatives
4. Choose one (and get ready to deploy it!)

Let me spend a few minutes on the last step: "get ready to deploy it." Sometimes we forget that a decision is made to put it into practice, that after the decision is made, it must first be properly communicated, and then the decision maker must initiate implementation. In fact, a decision is neither good nor bad in itself; it depends on the success of its application. An apparently good decision will go wrong if it is not executed well and (it could happen) a bad decision can turn into a good action if it is applied wisely. I will give an example:

Four MBA candidates, female engineers, developed one of the most brilliant business plans I had to evaluate. The project consisted of using drones to transport human organs from their warehouses to the medical centre that needed one for an urgent transplant. The compelling presentation showed deep and insightful study and a path to doing good business with it. The MBA candidates had even contacted a health agency that had given its strong support to the project. So the business school decided to hire the four engineers and tried to continue the project. In short, they were unable to overcome any of the difficulties that arose, such as the lack of legal coverage for drone flights or the complex management of airspace; neither were they able to keep the support of the health agency alive. After almost a year, the engineers gave up and, one by one, they quit. A decision with high expectations turned out to be an absolute failure due to the inability to implement it successfully.

Now, the four basic requirements of the process I pointed out above operate differently depending on the type of decision faced by managers, which brings us back to the three systems I discussed in section 2.3: System 1 (immediate thinking), System 2 (slow thinking) and In-between system (unconscious thinking). The interaction of the two areas – requirements of the process and systems of thought – will identify the main characteristics that any method applied to management decisions take into account:

1. UNDERSTANDING THE PROBLEM AND DEFINING THE OBJECTIVE/ OBJECTIVES WE WANT TO MEET WITH THE DECISION

System 1	Understanding the problem and defining the objectives are automatic and simultaneous
In-between System	The objective could change during the unconscious thinking
System 2	Usually, the objective either comes from a higher level or is defined by the decision maker as the starting point of the process

2. ASSESSING ONE'S OWN KNOWLEDGE AND/OR ACQUIRING *NEW* VALID KNOWLEDGE TO MAKE A CORRECT DECISION.

System 1	Knowledge is processed from the manager's experience while understanding the problem
In-between System	Knowledge is mainly processed during unconscious thinking
System 2	Knowledge is enhanced by managing information and gathering different points of view

3. IDENTIFYING THE ALTERNATIVES

System 1	There is not a proper analysis of alternatives. Heuristics takes the lead here
In-between System	There is an unconscious exploration of alternatives
System 2	Alternatives are ideally identified through teamwork

4. CHOOSE ONE (AND GET READY TO DEPLOY IT)

System 1	The decision is made based on the intuitive association of previous experiences
In-between System	The decision comes up once *the mind is ready*
System 2	The choice tends to be made by comparing the potential risks and benefits of each alternative

All this is interesting, but we must never forget that, when talking about managers, "there is more than one way to skin a cat," which is a colloquial way of saying that in terms of processes and methods, each manager tends to act in accordance with their personal style. Let me rewrite here a sentence by Derek S. Pugh and David J. Hickson already quoted in this book: "As long as there is management, there will be the problem of how to manage better. In one sense, attempts at answers to this problem will be as numerous as managers, for each will bring an individual approach to the task."

4.8 ERROR-ORIENTED ORGANIZATIONS

It does not seem that managers give too much relevance to this factor. In Q12, when I asked about the elements important to make a good decision, the items "A clear organizational chart and allocation of responsibilities," "The level of operational stress in the organization" and "The level of personal conflicts in the organization" fell into category D, the last one. In Q14, when I asked about the reasons that had actually caused the errors given in the survey, "The organization does not have a clear organizational chart" occupied the category C, so it is not considered a fundamental reason either.

In their article, "A Decision-Driven Organization,"[57] authors Marcia W. Blenko, Michael Mankins and Paul Rogers state that the "Organizational structure is not the only determinant of performance. In some cases, it is not even particularly important." They seem to agree with the survey's findings on the subject. They also point out that "A corporation's structure will produce better performance if and only if it improves the organization's ability to make and execute key decisions better and faster than competitors."

The survey may not cover all the implications of the 'organization factor,' though. There are certainly firms in which it is quite difficult to make good decisions. We have seen some throughout this book that did not have a clear definition of objectives or where internal conflicts of interest were glimpsed. Everyone knows corporations that use their organizational chart to distribute corporate power or to reward or punish the most loyal executives instead of assigning attributions and responsibilities; where mission, vision and strategies are blurred or unknown; where hierarchy seems the main decision criterion; where results are all that matter; where communication does not flow; where functions are not well established; and where a lack of clear decision process leads to awkward and inefficient decision patterns.

In the management mistakes list of the survey, I found some good examples showing that organizational problems were at the root of the errors:

6 Extreme lack of top-down communication in the restructuring of an area of the company.

10 Lack of coordination in a negotiation that involved two countries. They signed the deal in one of the markets, which affected the pending agreements in the other.

20 Leading an organization through decisions made on subjective judgments, political issues and personal relationships.

21 Not assigning tasks directly to certain team members and letting them decide who did what, which ultimately led to some tasks not being completed on time or even carried out at all.

23 Losing track of a project by not following its development and measuring the results of each phase.

33 Considering other areas of the company as enemies and acting accordingly.

43 Inefficiency and failure to meet the deadlines due to the lack of rigor in management procedures.

44 Misallocation of resources, starting a project that finally does not work, which generated problems in an entire area of the organization.

71 A project in which nobody was concerned about the team motivation, and everything was left to improvisation.

80 Not clearly explaining the goals and responsibilities of each person in a developing area.

Yes, organizations must design a work environment that favours a fluid decision-making process and eliminate all those factors that hinder it. According to research by McKinsey,[58] "Managers across a range of global companies gave strong signs of growing levels of frustration with broken decision-making processes, with the slow pace of decision-making deliberations, and with the uneven quality of decision-making outcomes. Fewer than half of the survey respondents say that decisions are timely, and 61% say that at least half the time spent making them is ineffective." The article gives several reasons for dissatisfaction: the lack of real debate, complicated processes, overreliance on consensus, unclear organizational roles, information overload and company cultures that undermine empowerment.

An organization means an arrangement of resources: things and people. It operates through an assignment of functions and tasks to be developed and executed. Between resources and actions, the ethereal universe of decisions beats. A smart first decision in any organization would be to focus on that universe and ensure that it runs smoothly and properly. I will discuss this further in Chapter 8.

4.9 NUMBERS: ENEMIES OR FRIENDS?

When I was in my early 20s and working as a corporate analyst, I was assigned to analyse the distribution expansion of the company I worked for. I designed a financial model to operate on pre-Excel Lotus 1, 2, 3 (*remember?*), and every time they wanted to open a new branch, agency or store, I did the calculations of the market potential, the projected income and expenses and the net present value (NPV) for a five-year period. After each report was completed, my boss would show it to the CEO. The decision process on the corporate expansion required a positive financial analysis as part of the dossier. I felt honoured to develop those studies and tried to be rigorous. However, each time the study did not reach a positive NPV, the CEO gave instructions to change whatever was necessary to make it positive. I soon realized that all the studies had to be positive, so I decided to save my boss trips and crunch the numbers until every analysis showed a favourable result.

More recently, I was working on a business plan for a start-up that would compete in the healthy snack market. We used three methods to make the sales forecast. First, we obtained the size of the market (which was not as obvious as it seems), and we applied the market share of some similar cases after a few years of operations; second, we conducted a market test and survey, the results of which we projected onto the entire segment population; and finally, we visited some food stores, explained the project to them, let them try the product and asked for a kind of monthly forecast. The range of results we got from the three methods was from a certain number to almost five times that amount.

Moreover, when shown the valuation of the project, the partners did not seem so satisfied. One of them asked why we had used a 12% discount rate. I replied that it was the fair value for the estimated level of risk. He asked for it to be lowered to 8% and suddenly the valuation grew by 50% – in two seconds. Then he asked to apply a 2% increase to the fifth year cash flow that we used in perpetuity to calculate the final value. And another two seconds later, the value of the project had already doubled; it was that easy.

Those are some of the many personal experiences of that kind that I could recall here. I remember some other grotesque examples of how senior executives handled numbers to support their decisions, interests or mere opinions. I guess most managers in most industries in most countries have been exposed to similar situations. However, the results of the survey I conducted do not assign to the numbers great relevance as a cause of decision errors.

In Q12, it lies in the third category far from the top positions as a factor that enables a good decision to be made; only 19 managers out of 86 believe it is critical and 43 that is fairly important. The answers would surely have been influenced by the profile of the manager and also by the type of management error. Looking at Q14, "Misleading calculations; bad work with numbers" and "The lack of a financial study" fall into the fourth and final category of the elements that actually caused the errors that managers gave as examples of bad decisions. In the list of management errors of the survey, I could find only one stark example of numbers as the cause of the management mistake:

64 | Making an organizational decision relying primarily on numbers.

The academic world has devoted much effort to developing quantitative techniques to help deal with decision-making, most of it related to the analysis of uncertainty. The complex mathematical formulations have not been widely disseminated in the corporate world and their application is restricted to specific cases and areas. In most organizations, the use of numbers varies depending on the area of expertise. In finance, they can be really complex and sometimes tricky. In engineering and operations, they are absolutely essential. In product design and marketing, they must be treated with care to set proper margins and prices. In setting goals, they must be subtle and fair to motivate staff. In strategy, they must be rigorous and honest or they can lead to major mistakes.

Numbers assist managers to make good decisions in four main moments:

a) When calculating or estimating the value of the alternatives. You can manage an ad campaign following the performance of each channel or action. You choose technical equipment from several after rating their benefits and confronting them with the costs. You change a process to get cost savings higher than the required expense. These seem like pretty straightforward cases where numbers help decision-making.

But if we talk about *estimating the value* of an alternative before a decision, things change. We have already seen the effects of small variations on some variables on the final value of an investment, for example. Moving the discount rate one point up or down causes relevant changes in the values and also in the subsequent decision to be taken. In the typical net present value method, there are some procedures for calculating perpetual value at the end of the analysis period that can lead to quite different results.

I remember a fancy section that *The Wall Street Journal* had in the 1990s. Every month, they made a (supposedly virtual) monkey throw darts to create a four-stock portfolio and invited a group of investment experts – with all their data screens, financial applications and awkward formulas – to create their ideal portfolio, too. Six months later, the paper checked the results. The monkey beat the experts half the time. In the financial world, some more serious, painful and well-known examples could be recalled that would question the correct use of numbers, such as the case of Lehman Brothers, which went bust as a triple A company (based on its numbers).

b) Setting goals: in section 4.1, I discussed how important objectives are (not so much as some might expect). Sometimes we talk about goals as synonyms for objectives, but here I rather understand a goal as a numeric expression of an objective. Is it always necessary to put a number on an objective? Does it lead us to make better decisions? Well, this is an interesting area for discussion and research. I know of some companies and people that do not lift a finger until they see a goal. They seem incapable of taking any action if they do not have a numerical reference – a target – to reach. I also know quite a few managers who spend most of their time tracking figures and goals as if that were their primary role in the organization.

I remember a bank that every year lagged behind its competitors in an important product line: bill discounting. So, one year, when working on the annual budget, the CEO requested that a figure be put on that product at the industry average level, which tripled the original amount. Despite timid complaints, the budget went ahead and the commercial division was obliged to pursue that goal. But no special measures were implemented, nothing changed in the conditions of the product, nor in the training of people, nor in the marketing campaigns, nor in the sales routines. The first budget review revealed massive failure to meet the target. So the goals were adjusted and the focus shifted to something else.

I also recall a firm where budgeting was a daily task. The department in charge made an annual budget and distributed the goals by areas, branches and segments. But the benefit units were allowed to propose changes in the assignment of goals throughout the year. It was not a formal permission but an informal *habit*. So they moved goals between areas by putting something else here and taking it out there. When the shift was difficult to explain, the budget department could move an operation to a so-called 'fictitious centre' so that, at the end of the year, the vast majority of areas, branches and segments met their goals, and they received their bonuses, regardless of whether the company could have declared bankruptcy.

You may be familiar with the '14 points for management' proposed by Professor W. Edwards Deming in his repeatedly mentioned book, *Out of the Crisis*. In that case, you may remember point 11 when he recommends "Eliminate management by objective. Eliminate management by numbers, numerical goals. Substitute leadership." Being a 'numbers man' himself, Deming's perspective is quite interesting. His main contributions to management had to do with the use of statistics to optimize industrial processes. However, he argued that sustainable competitiveness could only be achieved through knowledge, empowerment and leadership rather than relying on metrics and control. I love one of his sentences: "Management by numerical goals is an attempt to manage without knowledge."

c) Making forecasts: managers draw strategies. To do that, they need to make previsions on any key variable, both in terms of context (economy, industry, markets, social and customer needs ...) and internal organization (size, structure, strategy, market share, products, income, expenses, profits, performance ...). Numbers seem quite important when it comes to foreseeing the future.

I remember when the MARTINSA group decided to buy FADESA, both of them being construction corporations. MARTINSA, far smaller than FADESA at that time, launched a takeover bid that was accepted by 86.48% of the capital, including the 54% of the main stockholder and chairman. The cost of the transaction was €3,498 million. It was 2007 and, while the buyer believed that the business cycle would continue to grow, the seller anticipated that it was about to turn.

The conclusion of the operation was that the owner of FADESA became enormously rich while MAR-TINSA was declared insolvent the following year and finally liquidated a few years later; all because of their different economic perspectives.

"Surprisingly large and persistent errors in recent forecasts of GDP, inflation and unemployment have perplexed macroeconomists and policymakers for quite some time." You can read this sentence in an article[59] written by Scott Schuh to analyse the mistakes made by private institutions and try to understand why their forecasts have gone so far askew. The conclusion of the study is that "On average, macroeconomic forecasts are approximately unbiased, but they are inefficient and the forecast errors are characterized by improper correlation." It is not surprising that Part Two of Professor Taleb's book *The Black Swan* was titled "We Just Can't Predict" or that Chapter 10 has been called "The Scandal of Prediction."

d) Specific purposes: and managers can use numbers for many and very different purposes. Let me recall this small chain of luxury hotels that set their prices in three phases according to the distance between the dates of reservation and use: in the first phase, they offer premium prices until a minimum occupancy ratio is achieved; then they raised the price above the average and finally they raised or lowered it based on the booking pace and the remaining rooms. When I spoke with the chain manager, they were thinking of including the weather forecast in the system, as this is a key element for reservations. It is easy to understand that the whole process was based on historic data and predictions; I mean, on numbers. And it did work out.

Let me finish this section with a statement from Edwards Deming that I am especially fond of: "One cannot be successful on visible figures alone. Now of course, visible figures are important. There is payroll to meet, vendors to pay, taxes to pay, amortization, pension funds and contingency funds to meet. But he who would run his company on visible figures alone will in time have neither company nor figures. Actually, the most important figures that one needs for management are unknown or unknowable (Lloyd S. Nelson, p. 20), but successful management must nevertheless take account of them." To make a relevant decision, managers must take into account the vision of the organization, the objectives, the internal dynamics, the stakeholders affected inside and outside, their interests and positions, the prospects of the context, the corporate positioning, the impact on brand image, staff motivation, customer satisfaction and more. I could keep listing items for hours. Professor Deming is right: You cannot always put a number on those concepts.

So finally: are numbers friends or enemies of managers when making decisions? I would say they are friends but not the best ones, nor the most reliable.

4.10 COGNITIVE BIASES IN MANAGERS

People are more prone to make mistakes when they are tired;[60] I am sure we would all agree. Therefore, it would be fair to wonder whether it is sensible to allow managers to make important decisions when they are tired. We can also ask whether it is reasonable for managers to make important decisions under stress or when they have strong feelings about an open issue or when they are heavily influenced by the opinion of a third party, no matter how tenable.

You may be familiar with the popular "Israeli Lunch Judge"[61] study carried out in 2011. The abstract of the study at www.pnas.org states:

"Are judicial rulings based solely on laws and facts? Legal formalism holds that judges apply legal reasons to the facts of a case in a rational, mechanical, and deliberative manner. In contrast, legal realists argue that the rational application of legal reasons does not sufficiently explain the decisions of judges and that psychological, political, and social factors influence judicial rulings. We test the common caricature of realism that justice is 'what the judge ate for breakfast' in sequential parole decisions made by experienced judges. We record the judges' two daily food breaks, which result in segmenting the deliberations of the day into three distinct 'decision sessions.' We find that the percentage of favourable rulings drops gradually from ≈65% to nearly zero within each decision session and returns abruptly to ≈65% after a break. Our findings suggest that judicial rulings can be swayed by extraneous variables that should have no bearing on legal decisions."

I cannot think of any other activity than the law in which neutrality is more critical. However, Danziger, Levav and Avnaim-Pesso's study suggests that Israeli judges become less lenient in granting parole as lunch approaches and more lenient immediately after. According to these conclusions, lunch (hunger, haste and fatigue) has a large influence on their decisions. The judgments made immediately before lunch seem to have been too harsh.

Fatigue seems to provoke a cognitive bias when making decisions. You may like it or not, but cognitive biases[62] are common in the human mind (including that of managers!). We can define cognitive biases as systematic patterns of deviation from rational judgment. If I were the president of an organization, I should try to make rational judgment the main *resource* my managers use when making relevant decisions. This would mean that the factors affecting those decisions are evaluated in a neutral way without the influence of invisible elements that may distort the valuation. Some of the biases show more potential than others to alter the decision-making process. I have studied them and selected those that could damage managerial decisions most intensively. Here is the *menacing* list:

1. The Narrative Fallacy
    According to Nassim Taleb,[63] we humans tend to assign a simple and easy cause/effect relation to our knowledge, creating a sort of illusion of understanding. If, let's say,

property investment falls, it can be said that people are afraid of the evolution of the economy. If it grows, the same guys can argue that people want to act before recovery comes along. Our need to make sense of the world creates in our mind rational stories that, unfortunately, often have little to do with reality. By believing we can explain the events, we think we can foresee them. Because of the narrative fallacy, we tend to jump to a conclusion although we ignore how the elements of the problem interact with one another and the real consequences of any possible decision about it.

I clearly remember the case of a CEO who ran a fairly large company based on a few elementary assumptions. Being in the low phase of the economic cycle, he launched an intensive programme to reduce costs and reinforce sales teams. Once the cycle changed, the results improved. He assumed that the company had recovered thanks to his tactic. So whenever things did not go as expected, he ordered to cut overhead and strengthen the sales workforce. A kind of military campaign was launched to shift resources from the 'cost departments' to the 'revenue departments,' which caused a mess: some areas were dangerously undercapitalized while sales teams were overcrowded. I knew quite a few cases of talented people who were doing a good job in their positions and were transferred to branches where nobody had a clue what to do with them.

I recall another interesting example. In 2017, we celebrated the 25th anniversary of our MBA at IMD Business School. The guys organizing the gathering invited a professor to give a talk. They booked a classroom of a school owned by the husband of one of our classmates. The professor spoke for two hours about innovation as the absolute key to the competitiveness and survival of companies.

Through his presentation of more than 100 slides, he tried to convince us that in the following years nothing would be the same. Companies that could not introduce major innovations in their markets would be pushed out of the playing field. We were attending the talk in a traditional classroom of a traditional school, sitting on traditional chairs, taking notes with a traditional pen on a traditional notebook (he had brought them as a gift from the school), and the presentation itself was a very traditional one, projected on a traditional screen from a traditional projector. He even had to go back and forth slide by slide to find the message he wanted to convey at each moment. We bought his story because it was well articulated and, I believe, also because he had come to Amsterdam to teach for free. But his story involved a kind of narrative fallacy. Of course, innovation is important, but the correlation between dramatic innovations and performance is not damn high in all periods, products, companies and markets. There are quite a few competitive factors to take into account, and innovation is not always the main key.

If we can use a story, we save ourselves from analysing each element of a problem. The stories are easy to understand, recall and use. That's why we like them so much, even when they may mislead our conclusions or prevent us from taking critical elements into account.

2. The Availability-Misweighing Tendency
    We, including managers, tend to overestimate what we already know about a problem or objective and what is readily available to us. In his famous book, *Thinking, Fast and Slow*, Daniel Kahneman shows how the human brain tends to save resources. If you have what you consider a coherent association which can be used to solve

a problem, you use it. Professor Kahneman coins the acronym WYSIATI, which stands for "what you see is all there is" to express the overvaluation that we – managers included – assign to the things we already know – or think we know – about something. We tend to use the available information, no matter if it is scarce and irrelevant, and the knowledge we have, no matter if it is clearly insufficient or even misleading. This bias seems to be part of human nature: Moses Maimonides, born in 1135 and patriarch of Arabic-Spanish medicine, left written "The doctor's prayer," which included the following plea: "Remove from me the idea that I know everything and that I can do everything." He was aware of the WYSIATI bias almost nine centuries before it had been stated.

I consider the availability-misweighing tendency the mother of all the biases and one of the critical weaknesses of many senior executives and managers who decide through a mixture of urgency to act and self-reliance. Before a given situation, they tend to collect their immediate knowledge, sense that is enough to adopt a qualified stance and decide accordingly (pure heuristics). I have noticed that quite a number of them believe all they know about an issue is all they need to know. This thought or feeling leads them to ignore (at least to misweigh) some key factors that should be taken into account.

I could give dozens of examples of this widespread bias. I will choose one of the most extreme cases I have ever known. This guy was in charge of the so-called International Division. He had no idea of the complexity of the factors that operated in financial markets or the multiple technical items that made prices move, but he was arrogant enough to impose his point of view on the currencies prospects based on the little related information he was able to process and his slight and anecdotal knowledge of how things work in those markets. When the results were good, he boasted of his intuition and ability to grasp market trends. When the results were not good, he always found a victim to blame.

Sometimes, the impact of the availability-misweighing tendency is even reinforced by the effect of some complementary prejudices like the so-called Anchoring bias. The Anchoring bias shows the high importance of the first piece of information we acquire on a given topic. We – also managers – learn something specific about any matter and our mind can get an idea ('jump to a conclusion' to used Kahneman's words) from that little information, though it may be really tiny or partial. We learn, for example, that a company successfully used 3D printing in the manufacture of window frames (real case, by the way). So, we stay anchored in that positive information, and it will be difficult for us to change our mind about the favourable effect of 3D printing to ease the production processes.

3. The Overconfidence Effect

Another complementary prejudice that makes the availability-misweighing tendency even more serious is the so-called Kruger and Dunning bias,[64] which shows that ignorance often provides more confidence than knowledge. Some people – surely the majority – tend to hold overly favourable opinions about their own abilities. Not only do they come to wrong conclusions and make bad decisions, but their own incompetence prevents their mind from being aware of it. There are quite a few other prejudices and studies that confirm the tendency of people to overestimate their own abilities and capacities; obviously, managers are no strangers to this harmful illusion of superiority.

Yes, we believe we are better than our colleagues and our competitors. We believe we are more capable, more intelligent, more skilful, more talented, more effective and also more efficient. It is the prejudice known as the overconfidence effect. Many psychologists[65] have studied this phenomenon and have made interesting contributions. Their conclusions are that we trust our judgment more than reality would suggest and rely on the outcome of our actions and decisions more than we should. Sadly, our subjective confidence in our judgments does not correspond with their objective accuracy, which can lead us to make unsound decisions without the proper assessment of their most likely consequences. The overconfidence effect also makes us overlook the risks of our decisions.

I remember an interesting case that exemplifies this bias. I was hired to draw up a business plan for a project to design and manufacture three electric vehicles: a bus, a delivery van and an urban single-seater. The industrial Group developing the project had received 20 million euros for R&D from the public administration. The Group executives were determined to put the vehicles on the market in one year. They had bought a factory over 1,000 kilometres from the headquarters, where they drove at least twice a month (the CEO loved to drive at high speed). As soon as I began to analyse the project, I realized that it was lagging considerably behind the estimates of the Group owners. They had a bus prototype that was not even ready to test and had never travelled a single kilometre. The other two vehicles existed only on paper. I put on the table my opinion about the actual stage of the project that was quickly dismissed. Nevertheless, I decided to go ahead with the business plan. I made a valuation of between 50 and 60 million euros based on the situation at the time, but the promoters of the project expected something around 300 million euros. They insisted that the project was in its final phase, something clearly unrealistic, and had great business potential. I finally quit. Around a year later, I learned that the project had been dropped and the Group had sunk into a difficult financial situation.

By joining these three first biases (the narrative fallacy, the availability-misweighing tendency and the overconfidence effect), we could understand how the minds of many decision makers perform: they conjure up an illusion of reality, they believe what they know is enough to make the right decision, and they feel confident about the outcome. This thinking process in managers is one of the reasons behind many business mistakes. In fact, it causes decision makers to frequently overestimate the chances of success, underestimate the risk factor and miscalculate the inherent costs of projects.

Let's look now at some other relevant biases that reinforce the effect of these first three ones:

4. The Planning Fallacy[66]
    A sort of specific case of the overconfidence effect, the planning fallacy refers to the tendency of many managers to fall short on time estimates. Although experience warns that an activity or project will take longer than expected, they will insist on their optimistic deadlines and costs. The basic reason for the planning fallacy is a cognitive bias, but it's not always just that. Planners are often motivated by a desire for the plan to be accepted, so they tend to show the best-case scenario. By deceiving others, they also deceive themselves. Succumbing to the

planning fallacy will trigger a chain of new problems and the need to make new decisions under stress.

We could find thousands of examples of the planning fallacy. Let me pick a stunning one:

Construction of Berlin's Brandenburg Airport started in 2006, and the airport was originally expected to open in 2011. However, as of September 2019, no firm date for the opening had been set. After several delays, the work was over 2,500 days overdue. There had been serious issues with construction planning as well as project management. Additionally, the airport was well over budget, with an extra cost so far of €7 billion. The original budget was €2.4 billion. On top of that, some big problems had been reported concerning the fire protection system in Terminal 1, which might delay the opening of the airport beyond 2020.

5. The Confirmation Bias[67]

The confirmation bias is the tendency to seek information that somehow confirms our thoughts and to interpret opinions and events in support of our own ideas. Confirmatory data is considered highly reliable, while disconfirming data is treated with scepticism or directly questioned. A neutral decision maker will tend to seek information related to a particular issue or problem regardless of whether it supports or contradicts their prior thoughts. However, a decision maker affected by confirmation bias will interpret information in a way that favours their views, will remember only data or events that can justify their opinions, and will ignore all information that challenges their stance. To put it simply, in addition to being wrong, they stubbornly stick to their wrong conclusions.

Confirmation bias has a strong effect on negotiations and collective decisions as well. The whole point of the meetings and collective action is to reach a better solution through the interaction of different people with different experiences, backgrounds, knowledge and perspectives. But the confirmation bias causes us to adhere firmly to our first thoughts, overvalue the information that supports our point of view and undervalue the information that may be contrary to it. I have stressed several times the importance of flexibility for managers (I will insist on that); confirmation bias is a great enemy of flexibility.

6. The Endowment Effect[68]

As we saw in previous sections of the book, many decisions involve monetary valuations. Often, one has to decide whether to buy or sell an asset, a property, a right. To do this, the buyer and the seller must reach an agreement on the value. The decision is likely to be correct if they handle fair valuations. However, loss aversion bias[69] cautions us that we tend to consider losses larger than gains, although they may hold the same value. A decision based on biased evaluations will not be the best one.

The endowment effect is also related to the different valuations we attribute to things based on who owns them. Accordingly, managers under this bias tend to value their belongings over their market value, so they are not willing to sell them for their cash equivalent. The endowment effect implies that the maximum amount we are willing to pay for an asset will be lower than the minimum we will require to sell it once belongs to us. This bias has direct implications for investment and trading strategies, asset management and corporate and personal negotiations. We will not be able to make the right decisions involving money valuation unless we get rid of the endowment effect.

7. The Sunk-cost Fallacy[70]
The sunk-cost fallacy is the general tendency of managers to retain a position or insist on a situation due to the appreciation they make with respect to the investment or expense they incurred. They have spent an appreciable amount of money, devoted relevant time or committed valuable effort, and this can persuade them not to rectify even if rectification is the best decision.

Sticking to the established plan even when it has proven ineffective or inefficient could be an attempt to correct the cognitive dissonance of having spent time and money without obtaining the expected return. And this can happen in many areas: you may tend to hold stocks with heavy losses in your portfolio, even if the prospects are really bad; or you can keep using expensive software even if it did not serve its purpose when you bought it; or you can extend the contract of an unproductive employee after having trained them for a whole year. The sunk cost fallacy can be a constant interference in managers' work.

8. Emotional Biases[71]
The relationship between mind and feelings is undeniable. We behave as emotional beings. Some will be more prone than others to being guided by their feelings. However visible, emotional factors will always influence our decisions. That is not bad per se. There are decisions that must consider emotions carefully. This section refers to those decisions that are adversely affected by the personal biases of managers, to the emotions that distort

the neutrality desirable to make a sound managerial decision. We list below a selection of those factors:

a) The halo effect: it is mainly prompted by the image of a person or a company. There are factors that influence your predisposition toward a person's actions, opinions or decisions. This effect may be due to hierarchy, physical features, personality, apparent intelligence, quality of speech, and social or professional position. The same proposal will be received differently depending on whether it is presented, for example, by the CEO, a middle manager or a low-ranking collaborator. Very few managers are oblivious to that ethereal concept of charisma that is configured from trajectory and an uncertain set of ambiguous qualities. Sometimes the context also alters our level of acceptance. We tend to value a speaker's message more than that of a speech attendee. In short, you are more willing to buy the ideas of people you look up than those that come from people you do not admire.

b) The liking-hating tendency: complementary of the halo effect, the liking-hating tendency makes us ignore the faults of the people, products or companies we admire and, on the contrary, we tend to ignore the merits of those we do not like; we can even distort their actions to make them more reprehensible. It works like the confirmation bias.

c) The doubt avoidance tendency: we seemingly tend to erase any doubt in a problem analysis before making a decision, which can easily lead us to underestimate the risks and make a mistake. This has something to do with the overconfidence effect, though the root of the doubt avoidance tendency is not high self-esteem but the desire to easily work out a problem or situation.

d) The FOBO syndrome: in some ways it is the opposite of the doubt avoidance tendency. FOBO stands for *Fear of Better Options*, and it can lead managers to become paralysed before making a decision, no matter how small or very important it is. According to Patrick McGinnis, FOBO prevents managers from "actually committing to something, out of fear that we might choose something that was not the absolute perfect option."

e) The inconsistency avoidance tendency: also related to the confirmation bias, it refers to decisions that would contradict our own beliefs and habits. It is very common for managers to be influenced by their ideology, whether this is political, economic, social, religious or ethical. If a problem or situation touches on any of these essential ideas, the manager will tend to find a way to make a decision that agrees with them. Managers are likely to become reluctant to apply a correct decision that somehow goes against their deep feelings and beliefs.

f) Envy/jealousy tendency: envy is probably one of the most present human feelings in literature and also in history. It is believed that as early as the first century, Seneca had described the sage as "Content with his lot, whatever it be, without wishing for what he has not." Although they are not exactly the same, jealousy and envy have been the reasons behind many poor decisions over the years, especially, but not exclusively, in small or local settings. The aspirational bias is an interesting variation that makes us imitate those we admire in the hope of catching up with them. Many of the decisions that are made with the aim of growing and climbing up the ranks are related to aspirational bias.

g) The social proof tendency:[72] this is the tendency to think and act like a large group of people. Faced with a situation of uncertainty, some will tend to imitate the general selection, renouncing their own criteria and assuming those of the group. Many decision makers adopt this behaviour as a way to reduce risk; others because of their ignorance or lack of own alternatives. This type of bias is well known to marketers, who often apply it to consumer campaigns ('the bestselling device') and also in the investment arena. Take, for example, e-cigarette stores: thousands were opened before the dangers of vaping were known.

h) The FOMO syndrome, where FOMO stands for *Fear of Missing Out*: It was coined linked to social networks as an effect according to which some users do not want to miss anything that happens in their groups and anything that may become a viral or trending topic. It shows people's interest in being in the spotlight. In this sense, some managers hate not taking advantage of any opportunity that keeps them on display. They are afraid to step off the radar screen and try to get involved in whatever comes up, regardless the lack of information and analysis or the level of risk they take.

i) Stress-influence tendency: at the beginning of section 4.10, we learned how stress and fatigue can affect decisions (through the 'Israeli Lunch Judge' study). Once weary, our minds tend to use just heuristics. We make decisions based on simple prior associations. That is why Israeli judges reduced their parole releases. Under stress, adrenaline tends to produce faster and more extreme reactions. Some stress can improve performance, but acute stress often leads to mistakes. In general, it can be said that stress tends to increase the level of impact of the other biases.

Throughout my 30-plus-year career, I have encountered many examples of each of these emotional biases. In fact, I would venture to say that not many relevant decisions were free from the influence of emotional factors. The halo effect seems to me one of the most present biases in the performance of managers, and I consider it especially interesting: it is true that we suffer the consequences of the overconfidence effect, and we tend to believe that our own decisions are more correct than what reality seems to prove. But it is also certain that this trend observes a limit, which is the level of admiration for some others. We can feel overconfident in our decisions unless someone we admire speaks up and shows their own point of view.

The inconsistency avoidance tendency may be the other most damaging emotional bias for the neutrality required in decision-making. I remember this specific case: You know that in Europe quite a few local languages are still spoken together with what we shall call 'common national languages:' Gaelic and Irish in the UK and Ireland, Breton and Corsican in France, Sardinian in Italy, and Galician, Catalan and Basque in Spain, just to mention a few. I recall this organization that noticed it was losing affinity with its local and main market. The marketing division concluded that they should use the local language as the first code for communication with customers. Shortly after the implementation of the measure, the legal division called for a large meeting to expose the problems that the language change was causing. A short discussion was enough to reverse the measure and start using the local language only if a customer requested it. The company continued to lose the support of many local customers. The top managers could not speak the local language and had never shown any interest in the local culture, either. Their only cultural reference was the 'common national culture,' and this was the actual reason for the decision change. Later, it was learned that those 'problems' that the legal division had denounced were just two letters received from two elderly women.

I shall finish the review of cognitive biases with the so-called 'blind spot bias,' which is applicable to all the prejudices set out above.

9. The Blind Spot Bias

You, manager or executive, have read the above texts and may think: oh, interesting stuff applicable to many people but not to me. This is also human. It shows the existence of the last cognitive bias on the list. Because not admitting the imperfection of our own mind is a relevant prejudice in itself that prevents us from taking the necessary steps to reduce the effect of our cognitive weaknesses. If we become stubborn and insist on being immune to the mental tricks that humans suffer, we will not be able to accept that we need to change to make better decisions in our organizations and, to some extent, avoid decision errors that affect their competitiveness and results. Being a victim of blind spot bias may make you feel happier, but at some point, sooner or later, you will become, at the very least, unreliable in making important decisions.

Reina and others[73] conducted a suggestive experiment whose findings illustrate the effect of blind spot bias. Here are their interesting conclusions: "Intelligence agents make risky decisions routinely, with serious consequences for national security. Although common sense and most theories imply that experienced intelligence professionals should be less prone to irrational inconsistencies than college students, we show the opposite. Moreover, the growth of experience-based intuition predicts this developmental reversal. We presented intelligence agents, college students, and post-college adults with 30 risky-choice problems in gain and loss frames and then compared the three groups' decisions. The agents not only exhibited larger framing biases than the students, but also were more confident in their decisions."

Now, let's study a real business case. It will provide us with a better understanding of how cognitive biases influence the activity of managers:

David[i.] was the CTO of CGBank. He had been hired around 10 years before when he was director of the IT division of a global consulting company. Throughout his career, he had gained prestige as a dynamic, charismatic and adventurous executive always willing to try new solutions. Peter is the general manager of the Digital Channels Division at the Bank and in charge of the business activities running online. Before joining CGBank, Peter worked as a partner in a renowned international auditing company. CGBank occupies the 12th position in the Spanish financial sector.

Repsol is a Spanish multinational company in the oil and energy industry with more than 25,000 workers worldwide. It has a network of 3,500 gas stations in Spain. Jim had recently been appointed director of business development. One of his first projects was the design of a kiosk where the users of the gas stations could carry out some inquiries and transactions, such as buying movie tickets or paying bills. Repsol's main partner for the project was La Caixa, one of the leading Spanish financial groups and almost five times bigger than CGBank.

Repsol asked La Caixa to include a consumer credit function in the kiosk, but the bank did not consider it a good idea. Jim then approached David, his friend at CGBank, and proposed that his bank participate in the project. Jim knew that CGBank's digital solutions were highly appreciated within the sector. David received the proposal by Repsol with his typical enthusiasm, though he was not responsible for the business aspect of online banking. He had to talk to Peter, chief of the Digital Channels Division of the CGBank.

David told Peter about the advantages to participate in Repsol's project, the chance of having access to a network of 3,500 points of sales and the prestige of working hand-in-hand with La Caixa. Peter had just read an article that predicted a significant growth of consumer credit in Spain. So he totally bought David's proposal and called his closest associates to start the project. They did not agree about the potential of the kiosks and expected just a few credit applications each month. Furthermore, they pointed out that the quality of the operations would be very poor, with a high expected default ratio. Finally, they estimated a significant workload required to carry on all the necessary technical tasks.

In spite of the negative assessment by his colleagues, Peter decided to undertake the project, which turned out to be a complete flop on all counts. The technical developments went on endlessly, many operational problems arose and the level of security of the final process was low. Once they implemented the microcredits in the Repsol kiosk, barely any credit applications were received (as expected), and the profile of customers was very poor. Despite the disaster, nobody seemed to care about the evolution of the project and, at the end of the year, David and Peter received their large bonuses with no reproach. In fact, both remained in their positions some more years, making frequent mistakes of that kind.

i. All the names of this case are figurative.

Can we identify any cognitive bias in the decision made by the general manager of the Digital Channels Division of CGBank? Of course we can:

- The availability-misweighing tendency is present both in the behaviour of David and Peter. They adopt a stance with little and unsubstantial information.
- Peter represents an example of the anchorage bias when one of his reasons to push the project was the estimate of growth he had read about in a recent article.
- The overconfidence effect takes place again in both David and Peter.
- Peter is a reflection of the halo effect on David.
- Both David and Peter fall on the doubt avoidance tendency when they ignore all the difficulties they will cope with.
- They are also an example of the envy/jealousy tendency (or the aspirational bias) because they enjoy the idea of sharing a project with large corporations.
- Finally, both represent a clear case of FOMO syndrome.

The evidence on the adverse effects of the cognitive biases on the managerial decisions is recognized in the survey that I carried out. Participants place this element in the sixth position among the 16 reasons for the managerial error that they gave as an example. Moreover, I would say that cognitive biases might be behind many of the other causes as well. The underestimation of risks, which turned out to be the first reason for mistakes according to managers, may be caused by biases such as the availability-misweighing tendency or the overconfidence effect. If we take the second reason for mistakes, the profile of the manager, it is absolutely conditioned by the sensitivity toward cognitive biases. The inadequate consideration of context elements, the third reason for managerial errors according to the survey, could be provoked by the narrative fallacy, by the availability-misweighing tendency again or by other biases like stress-influence tendency, for example; and so on with some other causes.

Let me finish this long section with a quote from *East of Eden*, by Nobel laureate John Steinbeck (the words in parentheses are mine): "In human affairs of danger (*risk*) and delicacy successful conclusion is sharply limited by hurry (*stress*). So often men trip by being in a rush (*heuristics*). If one were properly to perform a difficult and subtle act (*complexity*), he should first inspect the end (*objective*) to be achieved and then, once he had accepted the end as desirable, he should forget it completely and concentrate solely on the means (*decision*). By this method he would not be moved to false action (*mistake*) by anxiety or hurry or fear (*biases*). Very few people learn this (*experience*)."

With the quote, I end the review of the main reasons behind the decision errors that managers often make. Up to now, I have been considering decision-making as an individual move, the choice made by one person although they might have intensively discussed the problem with their team or with some colleagues or external experts. As I have been saying throughout the book, in most cases, managerial decisions are a matter of one man or one woman. Sometimes, however, an organization may have a system in place that ensures that some decisions are made as a group; they require the intervention of several executives before the decision is considered finally taken. I am referring here to the so-called 'collective decisions,' which deserve a little attention (in Chapter 5).

TEAM DECISION-MAKING

The words *group* and *team* are not synonyms. A group is not necessarily a team, and a team is a group in which its members have an assigned role and a common goal. However, for the sake of this analysis, I am going to treat both terms as equivalent. I will discuss here how a group or team influences a management decision. If this influence is absolute, we would be talking about collaborative decisions.

Ubuntu is a good example of how one can integrate collaborative decisions into their behaviour. There is a beautiful story through which we can understand the concept:

> An anthropologist was studying the customs and culture of a particular African tribe. As part of the experience, he prepared the following exercise. He placed a basket of local fruit under a tree and gathered the children of the village. He drew a line in the dirt and explained the game: "When I give the signal, you have to run to the tree; whoever gets there first will win the basket of fruit." At the start, the children held hands and ran together to the tree. Then they sat around the basket and took the fruit as a group. The anthropologist asked them why they refused to compete, to which one of the girls replied: "How can one of us be happy if everyone else is sad?"

The Ubuntu concept, which means "I am because we are," refers to an African-rooted philosophy that is based on the premise that the human being alone is meaningless, since a person's life is built and developed thanks to the relationship with others. One of the proponents of this philosophy is Nobel Peace Prize winner Archbishop Desmond Tutu, who advocates seeking what connects us with others, knowing how to put ourselves in the other person's shoes and adopting a broad perspective in the face of any problem. He says: "The solitary human being is a contradiction in terms. Therefore, you seek to work for the common good because your humanity comes into its own in community, in belonging."

Archbishop Tutu's granddaughter, Mungi Ngomane, has published the book *Everyday Ubuntu, Living Better Together, the African Way,*[74] which could function as a leadership handbook for companies seeking to get every apple while maximizing the well-being of their people. In the book's preface, Desmond Tutu states that: "Everything we learn and experience in the world is through our relationships with other people. Therefore, we are called to examine our actions and thoughts, not just for what they will achieve for us, but for how they impact on others with whom we are in contact." A little further on, Ngomane reminds us of another African proverb that very well summarizes the strength of collaboration: "If you want to go quickly, go alone. If you want to go far, go together." She rejects the idea that a person can be self-made, because we are all interconnected. She advises not to be fooled by the myth of the self-made individual, as isolation is not an option; we will always need to rely on others to achieve our goals. And she believes that the workplace can be ruthless and that the Darwinian notion of survival of the fittest is as relevant as ever.

5.1 THE CONTRIBUTION OF THE TEAMS

In question 7 of the survey, I asked: How do you think important decisions of an organization should be made? More than two thirds (67.4%) answered: "After a thorough process of analysis and in agreement with colleagues who are competent with regard to the situation." Then in question 8 I asked: How do you think most of the important decisions of an organization are actually made? Only 17.4% answered: "After a thorough process of analysis and in agreement with the colleagues with a competent word in the situation." There is a major gap here between how managers think it should be and how they actually regard it.

Additionally, in the survey, managers give team-related factors in Q12, a medium relevance among the 24 key elements listed for making good decisions. The two factors ranked 9th and 13th as shown below:

9   The team and advisors of the decision maker

---

13   The tendency of the manager to make team decisions

We must understand 'decision team' as a flexible concept. It can be made up of the people under your management or the people around you with the proper knowledge. A team is not just the associates below your box on the org chart. You can view internal or external advisers as part of the team, a partner, a stakeholder, your own colleagues, perhaps your boss; in fact, you can include anyone you can contact by phone or a video call. It depends on what you need at all times, because you may want to feel confident enough before making an important decision. As we have seen in previous sections, it is inadvisable to adopt any relevant decision before having acquired the required knowledge in each case (I have verified it: 'knowledge' is one of the most repeated words in the book).

So, what are we demanding from our team when we face a significant decision? Well, several things:

1. Knowledge: If we are convinced about the fundamental role of knowledge to make good decisions, and we agree that 'team knowledge' is broader and deeper than 'individual knowledge,' we already understand how a decision team can affect the quality of the choices, especially if the team is made up of people with different backgrounds and abilities.

2. Numbers: In section 4.9, I discussed the potential contribution of numbers to some kinds of decisions, but also the risk of overestimating the importance of numerical calculations when making the final choice. The team can help both ways: it can bring numerical expertise to the discussion, but it can also apply rational scepticism to give the calculations proportional and not excessive weight in the decision.

3. Information: Collective memory – social memory – is superior to individual memory; that is a fact. Sometimes information from the past can become a relevant element in the decision. Also, we've already mentioned the dangers of dealing with too much or too little information. As a team, someone can carry out that critical task of debugging and selecting the critical pieces of information needed to make the right decision.

4. Alternatives: Faced with a problem, a situation or an objective, there are usually obvious alternatives to consider. Often, the best is not in the obvious but in a more elaborate, creative and innovative solution or response. Group dynamics frequently allow these types of possible alternatives to emerge, which would be more difficult to devise from an individual thought process. As a group, the team can improve ideas, develop them and also spot inconsistencies more easily. Provided the team maintains a positive attitude, the minds of the participants tend to expand through discussion and open to new and more intrepid alternatives.

5. Neutrality: Proper evaluation of the factors involved in a decision requires a neutral cause-effect study of the interrelationship between those elements and a neutral assessment of their potential influence on the outcome of the decision. We have already seen the many prejudices that a human being is exposed to before making a decision. The collective interaction that takes place within a team deters these biases from arising or, at the very least, lessens the chances of damaging the decision process.

6. Implementation: In section 2.1, I wrote: "A decision is not just a one-moment move. Instead, it is a trigger-point move. A decision starts a series of actions, first of which is communication. It is an exercise of making and transmission." Making the right decision does not imply success. Success is achieved when the decision is implemented correctly and sufficiently. If the decision is discussed in a group, it will be much better understood by the people who must implement it; if it is taken as a group, everyone will feel involved and will be more committed to its proper implementation.

Throughout the book, I have been trying to separate the process of preparing for the decision and the moment of the decision itself. And as we have just seen, during this process – objective, information, analysis, alternatives – it seems reasonable to affirm that a good team can help managers make good decisions. Now, the person in charge (there is always one) must take the last step: finally, they must choose what to do. They can make it individually or can take a collective approach, not only during the earlier stages of the process but also at the very final moment of the decision. A collective – or cooperative or collaborative – decision normally involves a mechanism (Group Decision Support Systems – GDSS) that ensures that the position of any person in the team/group is taken into account on equal conditions, though a tool like that is not absolutely necessary for the correct functioning of the group.

5.2 THREE MEANINGFUL CASES

Let's look at three real examples of group decisions to study this topic. It goes without saying that boards of directors are considered important decision-making bodies in companies. I have known how some of them operated. I will refer here to two that worked quite differently, plus another project-level team decision case.

CASE A:

This was a medium-sized bank. Every two weeks, the board of directors met to review the evolution of the organization and decide on the issues that each division head put on the table. They presented the proposals, a short time for discussion was opened in which everyone could give their opinion regardless of whether they had any knowledge about it and, after a while, three things could happen: a) the CEO did not give a damn and ordered the team to continue without making any decision; b) the CEO was not sure what should be done, so he asked to study the matter in more depth and bring it up again at the next meeting; and c) the CEO liked the proposal and gave authorization to move forward.

Once the board was over, the secretary drew up the respective minutes, trying to make sense of it and that was how things continued to run.

CASE B:

This concerns a telecommunications technology company that sells its products in more than 100 countries. Aside from regular meetings to follow up on general business, the board of directors meets whenever there is a relevant new project or important decision to make. They invite some of the staff involved in the matter and, sometimes, external advisers. An intense discussion ensues during which the directors present questions rather than opinions. If they agree that the outcome of the meeting was satisfactory, they call a new meeting to be held a few weeks later to close the points still open. They can invite a senior advisor to that second meeting. They repeat the same format as the first one and then the CEO summons the people most directly involved. After listening to them, he makes the final decision, which is the one, he believes, that coincides with the position of the majority.

CASE C:

I was familiar with an online project that, starting from scratch, got more than 50,000 clients and around 1.1 billion euros of direct business. The initial team consisted of young, inexperienced people led by a middle-aged executive with experience in totally unrelated areas. They devised a decision process based on several committees where the discussion was open and equal. At the end of the discussion, the head of the commission used this kind of formula: "We agree that the best solution is this, right?" And the decision was finally taken. I am 100% sure that the collaborative decision process played a fundamental role in the success of the project.

These are only three experiences, but they are quite significant. They show that collaborative decision-making works depending on the profile of the person in charge. In case A, the CEO was the classic prototype of the 'executive' profile, so he would never allow himself to lose control of the decision. In case B, the CEO was primarily 'analytical,' so he involved many people in a thorough process, although he kept the final move for himself. And in case C, the person in charge of the project, with a 'strategic' profile, was aware of the need for everyone to be involved in the decisions to be taken and implemented a genuine collective decision-making system; he did so without the need for any fancy tools or mechanisms.

I must add something relevant: while in cases B and C cognitive biases did not influence much in the decision-making process or the final decision, in case A biases could be found in an intense and influential way, such as the narrative fallacy, the confirmation bias, the halo effect, the liking/hating tendency, the inconsistency avoidance tendency or the social proof tendency. Thus, the manager in case A would tend to be closer to a *wrong manager* than those in cases B and C.

5.3 BEWARE OF DRAWBACKS

Once at this point, one could conclude that a collective decision is superior to an individual one. I would not say that so forcefully. It will depend on the people who participate in the decision and the patterns of operation of the group. After all, a group or a team is nothing else than a sum of individuals, each one with his or her own limitations. A decision group or team[75] must overcome quite a few elements that could distort the decision process. Factors such as unbalanced information, lack of freedom and confidence, unsettled direction, toxic participants or an unshared mind-set may cause the group dynamics to fail.

Here we have a recent example: this was a large meeting of managers, around 70, from a company with 5,900 employees. One of the topics to be discussed was the future of teleworking in the organization after the COVID-19 pandemic. The predominant position was in favour of returning to the office and leaving teleworking for specific purposes only. Someone suggested putting the issue to a secret ballot; the result was by far in favour of continuing to telework. It seems that most executives were afraid to publicly display a position contrary to that of the CEO, who was in favour of returning to the office. Thus, in this case, a tool was needed to ensure the neutrality of executive positions.

The above example leads me to issue a warning about what some call the HiPPO effect.[76] HiPPO here stands for *Highest Paid Person's Opinion* and refers to how the presence of a top executive can affect a group's dynamics. If one of these bigwigs is in the room, the rest of the participants may be afraid to speak and especially to express their honest point of view, because it may contradict that of the senior executive. Status disparities can feed the apparent uniformity of thought and erase the supposed advantages of the collective over the individual decisions.

Despite HiPPO, I tend to agree that a collective decision-making has got a higher probability of success than an individual one. But to confirm this, a decision team must meet some conditions. In his much cited book, *Out of the Crisis*, Professor Deming states: "Everyone can take part in a team. The aim of a team is to improve the input and the output of any stage. A team may well be composed of people from different staff areas. A team has a customer. Everyone on a team has a chance to contribute ideas, plans and figures; but anyone may expect to find some of his best ideas submerged by consensus of the team. He may have a chance on the later time around the cycle. A good team has a social memory."

BUSINESS SCHOOLS BEFORE DECISION-MAKING

Once I was admitted to the MBA programme at IMD Business School in 1992, they sent me two books: *Essentials of Accounting* and *The Art of Case Analysis*.[77] We were supposed to arrive knowing the fundamentals of the business code, that type of universal convention that leads us to use numerical rules to record what occurs in companies; I mean: accounting. On the other hand, we should also know the ins and outs of the main didactic tool of business schools, what some call the backbone of their system: the case study, raised to the level of *art* in the book they sent to us.

The Case Method[78] was born in the 1920s, so it is about to turn 100 years old. At that time, Harvard Business School detected the need to implement a new teaching system that would bring the student closer to the real world of business. HBS professors began to write short stories (or not so short) that described a particular position of a company and left questions about how to proceed from it. The idea was, and still is nowadays, that through real corporate cases, students would be able to process the facts of the case and, by discussion with their peers, would broaden their focus and discover new options that would enrich their learning experience. The case study is supposed to let the student think and decide like a manager. In fact, it is also considered a decision-making technique.

My experience at IMD was fully satisfactory, leaving aside the overwhelming costs to cover. My vision of the world changed and expanded thanks to the insights of people – very smart people indeed – coming from 35 nationalities. I learned the different ways of approaching business and life depending on one's background and culture. I pushed myself beyond the limits and felt the joy of sharing a common and demanding goal. And I made long-life friends – what else could I ask for?

Was it a completely different learning experience than university? It was in many ways. University gave me the knowledge of concepts and tools and in the business school I learned to put them in context. At university, we had to deal with precise solutions and in the business school we mainly handled alternatives. At university, we worked on paper; at IMD we mainly worked with colleagues. At university, we studied; in the business school we discussed. At university, we were too young and inexperienced to make relevant decisions; were we mature enough in the business school? I would ask something else: do business schools really prepare students, no matter how mature, to make decisions?

If we focus on our survey, the position of business schools may be in question. When we asked the managers about the elements required to make good decisions, "The professional education of the decision maker" was ranked at 23 out of the 24 elements, only above "Good luck." Of the 86 responses, just six think that professional education is critical for making good decisions and 26 that is fairly important. This data might encourage business schools to think about the opportunity to turn their model around.

I did my MBA at IMD in 1992. My daughter took her EMBA at ESADE in 2020–2021. I followed her programme closely and came to the conclusion that only three big things had changed between that period: now everything is easier because of communication technologies; marketing is more diverse and powerful due to digital channels; and the old tendency toward consulting is now toward entrepreneurship: The rest remains more or less the same. I was surprised by the similarity between the business cases and also in the content of the topics. Despite thousands of researchers studying business management, corporate administration, success stories, etc., the basics remain the same. It seems that there is nothing new to teach beyond technological advances. The bulk of the programmes have not changed at all. I suppose that if Neanderthal man had created a company during the Pleistocene, he would have thought about stuff like leadership, planning, finance, customer needs, efficiency and so on, just as in the 21st century. Well, I may be exaggerating a little ...

6.1 PROGRAMMES

I shall go back to that question I left unanswered before: do business schools really prepare students to make decisions? I was unsure in 1992, despite the fact that the two first modules of the 10 that made up the programme were entitled "The Process of Management Decision-making" and "Analytical Tools for Business Decisions." The most vivid memory I retain of decision-making is the study of the Cuban Missile Crisis Case and how to apply decision trees to situations like that. From that point on, I knew that decision trees, with all their ramifications and hypothesis and odds, would not be the most useful tool I was going to learn there.

In reviewing today's programmes, things seem have moved backward. I took a look at the MBA information displayed by IMD (*my* business school) and INSEAD, which ranks top in the *Financial Times* Global MBA Ranking 2021, and this is what I found (obviously, I do not mean to point the finger at these two business schools but take them as examples of the sector):

IMD presentation of the MBA Programme
Text download from the IMD webpage on 21 July 2021:
"The IMD MBA Program is an intimate, personalized leadership development experience delivering an unmatched emphasis on entrepreneurship, globalization and digitalization while equipping participants with the classic MBA toolkit.

Personalized Leadership Development: A year-long, transformational journey developing your global leadership skills and entrepreneurial mindset, preparing you for a fast-paced, evolving world.

Leadership dynamics: Gain the skills needed to address the challenges and ambiguities of business, and the understanding of your own individual leadership style, working with a variety of specialized Faculty.

Organizational behaviour: Consolidate your leadership skills and ability to respond to the global business transformations of today and tomorrow.

Research and target: Work with the career development team and partner with subject matter experts to craft a career strategy and create your vision and branding.

Prepare for global opportunities: Through a series of workshops and individual career advice, prepare yourself to network and interview with recruiters.

Go to market: Take advantage of dedicated networking and interview time to secure your future role through on and off-campus recruiting events with diverse, global companies.

Entrepreneurial mindset: Why is entrepreneurship an important part of an MBA? The stream explores skills involved in starting, acquiring, growing, rejuvenating and harvesting entrepreneurial businesses.

Entrepreneurial ventures: Work with early-stage, high-tech start-up ventures to strengthen your understanding of this environment and its challenges.

Entrepreneurs and leadership: The career path of many of our alumni includes entrepreneurship, read about some of their different experiences.

Accounting: Gain a toolkit for understanding, interpreting and designing internal financial reports as well as public external financial statements.

Business and society: Address the role of the corporation in today's global society, as well as the roles of key stakeholders such as NGOs, international organizations and governments.

Economics: Examine economic forces driving competition in industries and markets and the implications for business strategy and public policy.

Finance: Gain a sound foundation in concepts and methods of corporate finance and financial investments.

Marketing: Develop your marketing skills from capturing customer value to digital marketing and customer analytics.

Operations: A close view at how aligned operations and end-to-end supply chain management support a company's commercial strategy and its execution.

Strategy: Take the role of a general manager who needs to integrate across all functions of the firm and sustain a competitive advantage.

A holistic overview: You will complete an end-of-module integrative exercise and in order to continue to the next level, you will need to pass exams in all core courses."

Don't you think something is missing? Have you seen the word 'decision' in the text? I have not. However, I count up to seven mentions of 'leadership.' It seems that the ultimate purpose is to shape leaders regardless of whether they are capable of making the right decisions. And I'm sure everyone can remember some leaders known for the poor decisions they made. Let's now look at the INSEAD information taken literally from their full-time MBA programme brochure.

INSEAD presentation of the MBA Programme

Text obtained from brochure download from the INSEAD website on 21 July 2021:

"Consistently ranked amongst the top MBA programmes in the world by the Financial Times, there is a myriad of reasons why INSEAD's accelerated full-time 10-month MBA stands out from every other programme in the world:

Beyond Diversity: At INSEAD, everyone is a minority. With no dominant nationality in the class, you will be exposed to a world of new perspectives.

From Aspirations to Reality: Be it a career switch, advancement or new business venture, the INSEAD MBA helps our graduates realise their professional aspirations.

Agility and Resilience: The intensity of a 10-month program equips our students with the ability to multitask, respond to changes and tackle complex situations.

Global Community: The bonds fostered with one another during the programme often translate to lifelong friendships and business opportunities. You will join the INSEAD family of over 61,000 influential alumni in more than 175 countries.

Responsible Leadership: Through the Personal Leadership Development Programme, we empower students with the right expertise and mindsets to go out into their respective fields and create a positive impact on society, driving business as a force for good.

World-class Faculty & Research: With a wealth of experience and talent, our faculty creates top-notch programmes and cutting-edge research that influences businesses around the world.

One year to challenge your perspectives:

Period 0: Pre-MBA Elements: Business Foundations Week. Exploring Management Challenges. Language. Classes Webinars.

Period 1: Financial Accounting. Financial Markets & Valuation. Introduction to Strategy. Organisational Behaviour I. Prices & Markets. Uncertainty, Data & Judgement.

Period 2: Corporate Financial Policy Leadership Communication Foundations Managerial Accounting Managing Customer Value Organizational Behaviour II Process & Operations Management.

Period 3: Business & Society: Ethics, Political Environment, Public Policy. Macroeconomics in the Global Economy.

Periods 4 & 5: Electives.

Personal Leadership Development Programme: Throughout the curriculum, you will also go through the PLDP, designed to guide you toward heightened self-awareness through personalised coaching, interpersonal skills and effective communication.

Customise Your Programme: Elective Courses and Field Trips: From Period 3, INSEAD offers you an average of 90 electives. With a plethora of electives available, you will take learning beyond the classroom. Courses such as "Building Businesses in China" or "Building Businesses in Silicon Valley" are examples of field trips that give you the opportunity to meet a variety of alumni, entrepreneurs and executives in different countries, creating a unique hands-on experience."

Again, is there something missing? I know that not all skills provided by an MBA would have to be listed in the programme information, but the essentials should be there, right? If we asked managers about the basic skills necessary to become a good executive, don't you think that one of the most repeated, if not the most, would be the ability to make good decisions? Can you think of any other quality with more influence in an organization? However, you will not find the word 'decision' in the information of the MBA programmes of IMD or INSEAD, two of the main business schools in Europe and the world.

I did find professorial teams specialized in what they call 'decision science.' I went through their research and publications, and I encountered much university-like material, quite a few papers and articles developing numerical models to supposedly optimize decisions under certain conditions. They seemed to me typical theoretical lab studies, challenging and admirable, but hardly usable by managers.

It may be time to ask yourself whether research from top business schools and their programmes should include some of these 20 decision-related knowledge areas:

1. A business decision tends to be a complex operation: elements to be taken into account and different types of decisions

2. How logic should be applied in complex scenarios

3. How heuristics work in human mind; in which cases heuristics can be useful and in which cases inadvisable. The *extended* dual system of reasoning

4. The potential effect of unconscious thought in decision-making

5. What is the influence of ethics, beliefs and values on decisions

6. How to define a suitable objective; how to ensure the coherence of objectives along the organization; how stable or flexible objectives should be

7. How to assess if a decision is correct or not; the balance between outcome and process

8. How to combine short-term goals with long-term purpose

9. How to deal with the unpredictable

10. How to evaluate performance beyond the KPIs

11. The role of numbers in decision-making: how far can we trust them?

12. How to assess the risk behind a decision. How to achieve the right balance between risk and entrepreneurship. Being aware of the risk profiles of decision makers

13. Being aware of the general profiles as decision makers. Remember the Peter Principle

14. The figure of counterparts in any decision

15. The influence of context on decision-making

16. The key of the team to reach a correct decision. Individual versus group decisions

17. The adequate information before a relevant decision: quantity and quality. How to get reliable knowledge of the information

18. Warning on cognitive biases, especially the overconfidence effect, the availability-misweighing tendency, the confirmation bias, the inconsistency avoidance tendency or the halo effect

19. Communicating decisions and getting ready for their implementation

20. Decision-oriented versus error-oriented organizations

6.2 THE CASE METHOD

I have talked about the programmes. Now let me dig a little into that century-old tool essential in any business school on the planet: the Case Method. I have reread *The Art of Case Analysis* and realized that business cases are as similar to authentic management as dummies to human beings. They make up a parallel universe that has little to do with genuine reality, a universe with its own rules, processes and tricks. Let me highlight some of its features that I find questionable.

a) A case involves the description of a business situation. The information required for the discussion is selected, collected, processed and displayed by the authors of the case. They carry out an important part of what a manager's role should be: understanding context. And they do so by handling the information they deem appropriate. An MBA candidate will have to go through this process on their own after graduation.

b) The cases usually propose to the students the aspects they must focus on and expose the specific points to work out. It is like putting a magnifying glass on priorities to act on. Again, the author of the case takes over the job of the manager. By targeting an issue of interest, they tell the student what the relevant factors and the objectives of their actions are. Again, a true manager will never enjoy that ease in their company.

c) Business cases are mainly success stories. Not long ago, I was invited to attend an MBA class at one of the top five business schools in the *Financial Times* 2021 ranking. They discussed the Amazon case. Yes, Amazon, a unique corporation created at a unique time in unique circumstances. Amazon is a nonreplicable organization whose strategies are not easy to follow (and it is probably not advisable to do so, either) by any other company.

As I have argued, most business cases tell a success story. The author of the case builds a kind of report where everything tends to make sense. Although it is said that the cases do not have a certain solution, the final purpose is to obtain some conclusions, not always explicit, that explain the evolution of the company or the issue under discussion. The future seems predetermined by the forces acting on the organization, some in a positive way and others negative. The author's point of view is inexorably transferred to the narrative. I feel that many cases suffer from the so-called narrative fallacy that we saw in section 4.10, and I doubt that the decisions suggested in the discussion of the cases are transferable to other companies and other settings. Especially when hasty answers to complex problems are apparently permitted and speed seems to prevail over analysis.

d) Speaking of which, here is the core of this review on the role of business schools in decision-making. I copy a paragraph of the aforementioned book *The Art of Case Analysis*: "Your main objective is not only to read the case, but to comprehend its contents as efficiently as possible. Considerable emphasis is on 'efficiency' because time is generally a constraint. Other cases must be prepared, other papers written, other assignments completed. Consequently, an advantage accrues to the student who can read and comprehend a case in a minimum amount of time."

In an MBA everything has to be fast, with no time to waste, not even a minute to stop and ... think. The underlying message is: be quick whenever you need to make a decision, because other decisions lie ahead. When I was doing my MBA, we normally had to prepare three cases a day. I finished dinner around eight o'clock and spent four or five hours reading the 20–30 page cases that we would discuss the next day. We also had additional information available to help us understand what was going on in each case. Imagine the speed of reading and the depth of analysis.

It's kind of a paradox because they did not teach us (or my daughter 29 years later) anything about heuristics, but the whole system pushed us into the arms of heuristics. We read the cases without time to reflect, contrast, compare, estimate or project. To keep up the pace, you need to draw on your own experience and respond based on first impressions; therefore, the only possible reaction is through heuristics. I am sure teachers understood how complex the scenarios are, how difficult it is to collect information, how intricate a process it is to identify alternative solutions and how awkward it may be to evaluate them and make the final decision. Heuristics should not be the recommended practice in that situation, right?

I would dare to propose to the business schools that they rethink the method. As a first step, instead of writing stories, I would tell them to select both successes and failures, good and bad decisions, right and wrong strategies. They would only identify the organization, the background and the areas of expertise involved. They should then allow enough time for the students to build the case, understand the context, review the necessary information, interact with the affected people and detect where the problems lie. They could organize the group as a real team, with a leader and an expert per area. They would do the work from start to finish, and they would present their conclusions and proposed decisions to their classmates and teachers. Instead of three cases a day, assign a case every three days (or three weeks!). By doing so, students will never leave the real world and the learning experience is guaranteed. And they would be able to make real valid decisions afterward.

6.3 THE FINAL MASTER'S PROJECT

As one of the milestones of any MBA-EMBA, the Final Master's Project requires a lot of time from business school students. I have vivid memories of my final project at IMD. It was 1992, the Eastern European countries were just beginning their economic transformation, and we had to help a Triple-A Bank enter those markets that were opening. It was a real project in a real setting for a real client. We, a group of six people from Japan, Malaysia, Spain, Sweden, Switzerland and the United States, had real interlocutors who followed the project closely (we gave three presentations at their facilities in Zurich), because it was important to them and, in addition, they would have to pay a fee. I remember very well the last moments of the final presentation. We had submitted our analysis, everything had gone well so we were already feeling relaxed and happy. Then, after congratulating us, one of the bank managers asked, "And what will we do from here?" There was an awkward silence for a few seconds until a (brave) groupmate dared to reply. His first words were, "I'm not really sure, but my gut feeling is ..." It was like a punch to the face. In that moment I knew we had failed. Regardless of the grade we got (a B+ by the way) I knew that our work would not be useful because it did not lead to clear decisions. To top it all, I did not agree with my friend's gut feeling.

Today, the final project is usually the writing of a business plan. The economy has changed since 1992 and now demands more entrepreneurs than consultants. Business schools take up the challenge and adapt to the requirements: MBA-EMBA candidates will have to play the role of start-uppers and engineer a business project. Let me be blunt here: Anyone can write a business plan. You need an idea, a script, internet access, a telephone and be Excel literate; you must also write a consistent story (Kahneman would like this one). A business plan tends to be a fairy tale where everything looks pretty and cool, while reality seems more like Dungeons & Dragons, where a monster can pop up at any second. I will give you a good example to support my position.

This was the final project of an EMBA in one of the top European business schools that obtained the highest possible score. The plan was to produce 99% healthy doughs in their own bakery to sell in gourmet shops to young upper-middle-class families with children, who would love to bake the doughs at home as a family snack. The story sounded really good, and the presentation was just fantastic. And it was a real project! Three months later, once they tried to make it happen, it had switched to 100% natural donuts through outsourced production to sell to primary schools for the children's snack between meals. Another three months later, the market segment shifted completely again once they realized the costs would be much higher than they had calculated.

I think the only thing you learn from writing a business plan is writing a business plan. The true learning experience begins with the execution. It's easy to write a project, esti-mate sales and costs, imagine campaigns and simulate hiring, I mean, play the entrepreneur. It is unlikely that the main problems can be identified on paper. In the above project, they had to face great difficulties in each step of the value chain, from acquisition to marketing. Getting the right suppliers took weeks, testing the formula of the prod-ucts became a nightmare, costs calculation changed dra-matically, the production process turned really complicated due to health issues, especially in the dough cooling phase, and plans to set up a bakery were blown away due to a criti-cal factor that no one in the project jury detected: while the basic input in the pastry industry is flour, it is fruit and veg-etables to produce natural snacks. Nobody ever raised any question about a critical factor, the so-called water activity, which conditioned the production process, the distribution channels, the pricing and even some essential values of the product (the need for additives, for example).

I would suggest that business schools change the system here as well. The final project should be a true project, either helping new ventures or starting a new one on their own. That would be real-life experience, and it would give stu-dents the useful clues they need once they get out of school. If business schools assume the need to change the system, they will probably also have to transform their organization and reshape their resources; it would be a challenging deci-sion for them.

HOW MANAGERS CAN AVOID MISTAKES

Think of your ideal manager, the perfect executive, capable of tackling any position or assignment and meeting objectives no matter how difficult and cumbersome they may be. I do not think you are imagining a financial master, or a marketing star, or a fearless entrepreneur, or a savvy technologist or a sly strategist. Rather of thinking about any hard skill or area of expertise, you will tend to highlight soft general abilities like motivation, communication, vision, maybe even analytic skills. Now I would like to ask you to list in your mind the skills that the most successful managers usually have. 'Successful manager' is not synonymous with 'ideal manager,' right? Managers can be successful in the sense of being recognized despite their poor performance. It is an uneasy thought, a wrong but successful manager, though I am sure we all have known a few cases of those.

So I also asked some top executives to tell me what they considered essential skills to become a successful manager. They were informal conversations; I let them talk without a guide or closed answers. One of the common ideas was that successful managers usually possess a certain degree of charisma. Such an abstract concept ... It could be defined as a quality that generates attraction and the ability to interact with key people: a person with charisma ends up becoming part of the community of *winners*. I guess they identified a successful manager as a leader, just as some business schools tend also to do. However, the most repeated idea, expressed in their own words, was a sort of two-way empathy. They observed that upward and downward empathy was the authentic clue to becoming a successful manager: on the one hand, the ability to gain the trust of bosses and colleagues; on the other hand, the ability to be admired and followed by associates.

Charisma and empathy: You can hardly learn those skills in college or business school. It would be fair to ask whether universities or business schools can teach you how to become a successful manager.

We know that in the assessment of oneself, there are at least three versions: the genuine reality, your own version and the version perceived by others. Applying these three scopes to the quality of ideal managers versus successful managers, I identified eight relevant different combinations. Let's remember the concepts before deploying the options: an ideal manager would be able to meet the objectives; a successful manager would be the one who gained recognition from their peers. Here are the combinations:

WHAT KIND OF MANAGER I REALLY AM	WHAT KIND OF MANAGER I THINK I AM	WHAT KIND OF MANAGER THEY THINK I AM	POSSIBLE CONCLUSIONS
Neither ideal nor successful	Ideal and successful	Neither ideal nor successful	I have a big problem and need a coach or something
Ideal but not successful	Ideal and successful	Ideal but not successful	I need to improve my attitude, my communication or possibly both
Ideal but not successful	Ideal but not successful	Ideal but not successful	I need to trust somebody to help me improve my image in the organization
Ideal but not successful	Ideal and successful	Neither ideal nor successful	I better find a new place

WHAT KIND OF MANAGER I REALLY AM	WHAT KIND OF MANAGER I THINK I AM	WHAT KIND OF MANAGER THEY THINK I AM	POSSIBLE CONCLUSIONS
Not ideal but successful	Ideal and successful	Not ideal nor successful	I should think about improving performance and possibly moving to a new company
Ideal and successful	Ideal and successful	Not ideal but successful	I should try to improve my attitude in the company
Ideal and successful	Ideal and successful	Ideal but not successful	I should try to improve my interaction with my peers
Ideal and successful	Ideal and successful	Ideal and successful	Everything is okay

The table above is subject to new combinations and many possible interpretations. We would agree that the latter is the optimal level, the objective desired by any manager. We would also agree that it is not that easy to achieve; we not only wish to become good managers but also to be recognized by others as such. We may need knowledge, experience, the right context, the correct attitude ... I'll tell you something: above all, we need the ability to make good decisions, and I'll explain why.

The difference between an ideal and a wrong manager mainly lies in the quality of their decisions (in section 3.3, I discussed what a correct decision was). The good decisions of managers meet the objectives set by the organization, so they contribute to what the organization tries to achieve. The ability to make good decisions can be applied to finance, marketing, technology, strategy or any area of the organization. Good decisions can also be transferred to motivation, communication, vision or any aspect of management in the organization. And good decisions help managers gain the recognition of their bosses, the respect of their colleagues and the admiration of their associates. If you make the right decisions, you will be a good manager and it will be also easier for you to become a successful manager.

The first concern of managers should be how to make the right decisions. Many managers would need a real twist in the way they do things to steer it toward decision-making. You want to make the right decisions, especially the most critical ones. You do not want to make a mistake out of haste or ignorance or because you were not ready yet, or because you missed a key element, or because you underestimated the risks, or because a previous experience misled you. There can be so many forces pushing and pulling you in different directions that it's easy to feel overwhelmed and ultimately make a mistake. What can you do when everything seems simply too complex, or the context becomes too noisy, or your boss demands a quick response or your mind seems unable to handle so many factors? In those cases, you need to achieve a position of neutrality that frees you from all the hazards and menaces.

Neutrality means excluding biases and prejudices in decision-making and, therefore, being able to decide objectively and impartially, always under the values established by your organization. The organization's values outline the framework in which you should apply neutrality. The neutrality will allow you to detect all the faces of a subject and take into account in a fair way the nuances of its analysis with the values of the organization as a fixed factor. In other words, if you want to increase the chances that your decisions will be considered correct, you must ensure that you assess fairly all the elements that will influence the outcome of the decision according to the general criteria of your organization.

The question is how you can achieve that required neutrality when everything seems to be against it. I will give you some clues in the following sections drawn from the analysis I have done over the past few years.

7.1 MANAGERS NEED A METHOD

In the decision-making classes I delivered, I used to show the following process chart. Before showing it, I asked attendees to think about an efficient decision-making process. They came up with a sequenced series of tasks as valid as my own. And we discussed for a while which task was more essential than others and what would be the perfect order. By the end of class, everyone felt that we had done a good job coming up with a sensible recipe that would help us make better decisions. Then we went back to our offices and forgot which step came first and which came next. I'll be honest: that class, and of course the graph on the next page, were completely pointless.

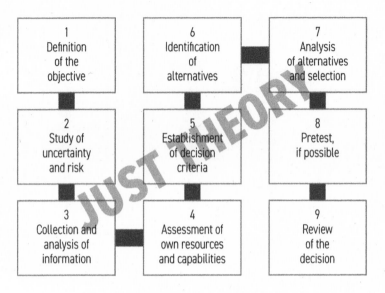

FIGURE 10: A THEORETICAL DECISION-MAKING PROCESS

I will not waste your time going through that path because I'm sure you will never use it. You are a unique manager, and you act according to your unique profile and experience. You do not need a utopian process of magic effects. There is no such thing, and you would never internalize it. You do not need a process but a method, which is something different. If you want to refine the way you make decisions to improve your chances of being right (that is what this is all about), there are a few things to consider that I bring up here from the earlier reflections set forth throughout the book. Notice that they are not steps of a process but clues to devise your own method:

1. Ask yourself: is this a decision with potentially significant consequences that forces me to focus on its analysis, or is it a minor issue where a mistake would not have

a serious effect? If you conclude that the decision is a relevant one, you should prepare to spend time and energy on making the right decision. If otherwise, you can follow Gary Klein's RPD model[79] (Recognition-Primed Decision Model) that suggests using your previous knowledge to find a quick and good-enough solution to a problem by acting based on clues like those below:

- The focus must be on assessing if the situation is familiar, not on comparing alternatives
- Courses of action will be quickly evaluated by picturing them implemented, not by thorough analysis
- Decision makers grasp the first workable option they find, not the best one
- The emphasis is on being poised to act

I recommend this type of behaviour recipe only for those minor decisions whose effects in case of failure would be controllable and never serious. The rest of the clues are for the relevant decisions you will have to face.

2. Decision makers tend to focus only on a small part of the scenario, the one that directly affects the problem, and they often neglect the broad perspective of the organization. Because your decision is embedded in a complex system where all factors are interconnected, you should never lose sight of the big picture. The first of those factors is the overall purposes of your organization; the second, its strategic objectives.

You must always keep in mind that your position is just one piece of something bigger, and therefore your decisions must be influenced and will influence the rest of the pieces and all of them as a whole. A right solution for you or your unit may not be as convenient for the organization; sometimes it can also go against its main objectives and strategies. As a good manager, you do not want that to happen.

3. Do not take the objective of a decision necessarily for granted. You cannot go against objectives, but you can certainly discuss, refine or at least clarify them. We have seen that some failures in management come from poorly defined objectives, which sometimes were not even established in coherence with the logic or the general strategy of the organization.

    Make sure that the objectives to be met by the required decision are clear to everyone involved in the decision and shared without conflicts of interest. Also be honest enough to see if the objective is compatible with your own personal goals; otherwise, you better avoid the decision until you're sure that your personal position does not interfere in the eventual decision.

    Try to emplace the objective in the short, medium and long term and enhance the long perspective before making your decision. Take care that the objective is in the direction indicated by the mission or purpose of your organization, division and unit.

4. Think about whether the context of the decision is certain or uncertain. A certain context implies the existence of implicit or explicit data that will allow you to evaluate the result of each possible action. In that case, it is likely that you can convert the problem into a numerical calculation – sometimes you will need technical assistance – and therefore choose the best option, which will be the one with the best value. However, I am afraid that most of the situations will entail an uncertain context, so you

will need to be prepared for a thorough analysis beyond any possible numerical solution.

5. Do not rush; restrain your temptation to respond as soon as someone asks you for your decision. Let your mind work on its own for a while. It will soon improve the decision you would make on impulse. In other words, embrace unconscious thinking – it will pay off.

   Do not stick to obvious solutions either. Discuss the problem with your associates and ask for the opinions of people with experience in various areas. Make the elements involved in the decision interact and seek a broad perspective. You can even undertake a creativity exercise if you think the case may be appropriate. By doing all this, you are very likely to improve any obvious decision.

6. Here comes one of the most critical points in making a good decision: a complex situation under uncertain circumstances will not allow you to ignore any of the key elements involved in the case. If you ignore or do not realize an important factor, the chances of being wrong will skyrocket. What elements are those you cannot miss? I will give you a short list:
   a) Economic, industrial and social trends. In principle, it does not seem wise to make a decision against the current. On the contrary, the decision is likely to be more accurate if it goes in the direction of the business cycle (for example, investing with growth forecasts), industry tendencies, and social habits and needs. I'm not saying you cannot make a decision against trends; what I mean is that you must be aware of this and its possible effects when making the decision.

b) Risks. Any decision is a risk, and you cannot ignore the risks that the decision will incur. They may be of all kinds: on the viability of the company, on its image, on costs or efficiency, on employee motivation, etc.; we also have market risk, credit risk, operational risk, technological risk, legal risk, ethical risk. A fair assessment must be made of the possibilities of these risks occurring, an estimate of the possible consequences of their materialization and an approach to what is the best solution to deal with them. From the midpoint of equanimity, you decide whether it is reasonable to take the risk.

c) Counterparts. Your decision can become a trigger for other people to react, inside or outside the organization. That is why you must prevent possible effects or reactions from them once the decision has been made. Think about the stakeholders (individuals or groups) that may be affected and try to imagine their reaction to any of the available alternatives before making your final choice. Very often, the main 'counterpart' that should not be ignored is the clients. If your decision can have any influence on their expectations, you better study how your customers may take it.

d) Resources and capabilities. You and your organization count on some resources that you try to make the most of. But we know that they are not unlimited. Deciding to do everything is not an alternative. You have resources (people, technology, facilities, money, etc.) to which to assign tasks and projects; and you have capabilities (production, distribution, innovation, communication, etc.) that allow you to develop them for better or worse. The resources and capabilities of an organization outline a kind of perimeter in which it must embed its decisions. Making a decision that does not fit within that perimeter will likely lead you into error territory.

The 'overvaluation of the organization's capabilities' considered in the survey as a cause of error is closely linked to the "overconfidence effect" we have seen in the section on cognitive biases. Guided by this bias, some managers overvalue their organization's resources and/or undervalue the requirements of a task or project. It is important to bear it in mind when making a management decision.

7. The criteria are important. You do not want to base your decision primarily on intuition. Of course, your experience and knowledge are there, but the best way to use them is through criteria. Before identifying the alternatives to choose from, you must establish some criteria to guide your analysis. Imagine that the objective is to reduce the level of absenteeism by 25%. You can request that the possible measures be progressive, that they do not affect the work climate and do not cause a cost of more than 30% of the savings obtained. The alternatives you would take into consideration should meet those criteria.

The criteria will help streamline the thinking process, improve coordination within the decision group and facilitate communication of decisions once made. Through criteria, you gain fluency in decision-making and consistency as a manager.

8. Get ready for implementation. The decision method you devise must take into account the implementation of the decision to make. Imagine how you will communicate

your decision and how you would implement it. Picture in your mind the effects of your decision once executed. That will help you to assess the chances of success. If you do not feel confident enough on envisioning the communication of the decision to your peers or associates, you'd better have a rethink. If you do not see a clear path to put your decision into practice, you should review the factors that led you to make that choice. And if new questions arise when you envision the practical consequences once the decision is implemented on the ground, you may want to start over.

Some managers hate doubts, but I would appreciate reasonable doubts: they can lead you to make better decisions. By visualizing your decision in practice, you will not only be able to review the reasoning behind the decision to be made, but you will also have the opportunity to refine your chosen alternative of action.

These recommendations are conclusions drawn from the previous sections of the book. You may have missed 'information gathering' as a critical part of your decision method. As I said before, I prefer to point to knowledge as a key requirement. This will be discussed in the next section.

7.2 NO KNOWLEDGE, NO DECISION

The difference between a decision and a bet is knowledge. My recommendation is that you do not make any important decisions until you have acquired the necessary knowledge. Managers must learn to wait. No matter how strong the pressures may be, your determination must be just as strong. If you want to make a good decision, something especially desirable when you are faced with a relevant one, there is no other method than to acquire the necessary knowledge that will allow you to fairly identify and evaluate the possible alternatives. And that may take a while.

Managers can be tempted to confuse information for knowledge. But most of the time, information itself is just a compiled set of data and facts that must be processed to become knowledge. And that *process* involves receiving, understanding, discovering and learning. The information is there for you, but you must apprehend it to be able to understand its meaning, draw the appropriate conclusions and find out how it can affect the problem or situation you must work out; also, to interiorize it for future use. Then you will contrast it with your experience (previous knowledge) as well as with your values and those of your organization. This final step will put you in the position of being able to fairly judge the problem and evaluate the alternatives of solution; therefore, you will be prepared to make the right decision.

The inclusion of values[80] in the process of turning information into knowledge means that knowledge is not a precise concept that works in a uniform way. Knowledge is personal and its practical definition will depend not only on the individual values of the decision maker and the collective values of their organization but also on their background (accrued knowledge: past experiences influence on the present ones) and on their capabilities. No two people have the same abilities and show the same affinities. Each person's values will affect what that person attends to and thinks about, how they understand a situation and interpret and remember the facts. Thus, each individual is more or less prone to each area of knowledge.

The cement that unites all parts of the process is 'critical thinking,' the foundations of which were established by Diane F. Halpern in her book *Thought and Knowledge: Introduction of Critical Thinking*.[81] According to Professor Halpern, critical thinking is essential for solving problems, drawing conclusions and making decisions. Also for distinguishing between the important and the accessory in a society that evolves on the basis of information and knowledge. I would change the name of critical thinking and propose 'effortful thinking' instead. Why is that? Well, critical thinking requires a person to be able to (the list is drawn from Ms. Halperns' aforementioned book):

a) seek out contradictory evidence

b) use the metacognitive knowledge that allows novices to monitor their own performance and to decide when additional help is needed

c) make risk/benefit assessments

d) generate a reasoned method for selecting between several possible courses of actions

e) give reasons for choices as well as varying the style and amount of detail in explanations depending on who is receiving the information

f) recall relevant information when it is needed

g) use skills for learning new techniques efficiently and relate new knowledge to information that was previously learned

h) use numerical information, including the ability to think probabilistically and express thoughts numerically

i) understand basic research principles

j) demonstrate an advanced ability to read and write complex prose

k) present a coherent and persuasive argument on a controversial, contemporary topic

l) use matrices and other diagrams for communication

m) synthesize information from a variety of sources

n) determine credibility and use this information in formulating and communicating decisions.

Let me stop for a few minutes at points 'e' and 'f.' In 'e,' Ms. Halpern says to "give reasons for choices ..." I would like to add that those reasons must be determined in advance. I could call them 'criteria.' I mean, not only when identifying alternatives (section 7.1) but also before making your choice, you must first think about what would be the rules that will guide you to pick one alternative from all those available. I will return to the question of criteria in section 7.6.

The other point I would like to mention is 'f': "recall relevant information when it is needed." This is a good short sentence. As we already saw in section 4.5, being conscious of the relevant information you need to make up your mind is one of the keys in management decisions. In fact, on some occasions, no information at all will be required because your prior knowledge is sufficient to select the right course of action to take.

Looking at the whole range of requirements of critical thinking, we realize that it requires managers to be truly on task and committed to a continuous effort to get the best out of the process, which is by no means easy. External circumstances and the personal conditions of each moment make it challenging. Think about whether you can maintain that optimal permanent disposition when making decisions.

For a better understanding of the process through which to turn information into knowledge, I have drawn the chart below.

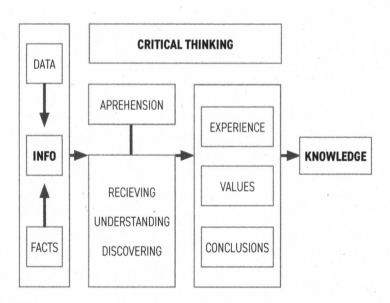

FIGURE 11: PROCESS TO TURN INFORMATION INTO KNOWLEDGE

Now a question: just as there are good and bad decisions, is there good and bad knowledge? Let's bring here a meaningful case that happened in August 2021, when he United States withdrew its troops from Afghanistan. One must assume that such a huge decision was made after enormous work to obtain all the information required to avoid tragic consequences. However, the entire operation was a complete disaster and the Taliban seized power after only 11 days of a smooth military campaign. No one can predict future events, but there is enough data to ensure that the decision was simply catastrophic in terms of the US's global image, geostrategy, democracy, respect for life, civil rights and culture. This terrible case proves that, after all, there certainly is something we might call 'bad knowledge.'

Good or bad knowledge has to do with reliability. How can you, a manager, be sure that the knowledge you have acquired at a given time is reliable and sufficient to make an important decision? Bad news: you cannot. What you can and should do is try to increase the chances of making a good decision by resorting to reliable knowledge and that happens under some conditions:

- Acquiring knowledge should be a continuous process. If you have accumulated information on a day-to-day basis and have been constantly reflective of the critical issues that affect your work and organization, you are more likely to be right in handling a complex topic than if you had to study it from scratch and quickly.

  The attitude toward continuous knowledge can be articulated in part through training and attendance at professional events, such as congresses or sectoral reunions. It is curious to see how some managers tend to send their associates to training and sessions especially on new content, while they are reluctant to attend these types of events, thinking that they are typically useful for lower levels of the organizational chart. I believe it's not the right attitude.

- The closer the source is to the origin, the more reliable the knowledge will be. In other words: the more intermediaries you put in the process, the less reliable the knowledge becomes. I'll give you an example: as a young manager, I was in charge of the 'industry analysis' of my company as an input for the investment strategy. We subscribed to various study services, compiled reports from many industry associations, maintained an archive of magazine news, built a large data file from various databases and so on. We followed a list of almost 100 industries and had a plan to write a report on each one in three years, which was not possible. Each report took us over a month and the team was small. So we decided to shorten the process by choosing four or five people from each industry whom we interviewed from a standard form. From that point on, each analyst could write a report per week and, more importantly, the content was much more reliable than before.

- Sometimes you may want to cross-check the knowledge you reached: just as you normally request a quote from more than one supplier, or a proposal from more than one potential consultant, or even more than one possible solution to a problem, you can ask for insight from more than one source, especially when dealing with a complex or sensitive issue. Has it been verified? How far is it verified? These are two questions that you may want to ask on some occasions, and you must develop the sense to answer them because each case has its own answer.

Remember the first months of COVID-19 in the world? The World Health Organization established that the pandemic spread through droplets, despite some qualified scientists bellowing out it was through aerosols.[82] Following the WHO recommendations, people began to wear gloves, apply hydro-alcoholic gel, wash their hands every minute, disinfect rooms and public places and almost burn their clothes in the washing machine. Much worse than that, people in many countries did not wear masks because, according to the WHO, COVID-19 particles were not suspended in the air. Not listening for months to the scientists who referred to aerosols, not having verified their knowledge in due time, was a management mistake with enormous consequences.

From the general to the particular: knowledge is a really wide and abstract concept, and this book discusses management. So which kind of knowledge are we referring to here? Let me recover Professor Deming's concept of 'profound knowledge'[83] based on the consideration of a company as a system, which must be understood as "a network of interdependent components that work together to try to accomplish the aim of the system." According to Deming, the system of profound knowledge will provide a lens enabling individuals to judge their own decisions, understand their organizations and ultimately optimize them. The implication for managers is the need to develop a thinking process capable of determining the future of their companies and not to be victims of the context. They must become lifelong learners and constantly explore "the environment (technical, social, economic) to perceive the need for innovation, new product, new service or innovation of method."

The bottom line is that managers must be prepared. They need to know what is going on around them and what may happen in the short, medium and long term to be able to face any circumstance or eventuality. Then each problem, each decision to be made, will require a specific search for information in pursuit of the consequent knowledge, but all integrated into the general system that managers need to know profoundly.

If you, as a manager, want to be prepared to make good decisions, you must take all the necessary actions to have a fair and updated knowledge of:

a) The economic cycle and the outlook for the coming years at the global, national and regional levels. Prospects for local and international trade

b) Social trends, those issues that most concern the world, national and regional population

c) Possible impact of the evolution of the environment on your industry and organization

d) Possible impact of the evolution of technology on your industry and organization

e) The habits, needs and motivations of your organization's customers and their perception on its image, values, products and service

f) How your industry works, the key success factors required to compete and what trends can shape its future evolution

g) The operating conditions, characteristics and limitations in each step of the value chain of your organization, from raw materials, if any, to post-service and customer loyalty

h) The strategies and capabilities of major competitors, as well as potential newcomers to your market

i) The position and interests of the key stakeholders in your industry and organization, including partners, investors, suppliers, policymakers and media

j) The purpose (mission and vision) of your organization, its general strategy, main tactic lines and its values (the real ones, not those that hang from some walls)

k) The motivations of the people of the organization; the work climate and the possible causes of conflict

l) The company's resources and capabilities, a hint of the kind of plans and projects the organization might be able to tackle

m) The weaknesses and strengths of your unit, what you as a team are better at and not so good at. The affinity of your associates toward the organization, the real work climate in your unit and the possible causes of conflict

n) Finally, the interests, beliefs and motivations of your peers and the associates in your area of responsibility

Nobody ever said that being a manager is an easy thing. You should reflect on your knowledge in any of those previous fields and how you can fill the possible gaps. You could still make a good decision even if your knowledge in any of those aspects falls below optimal, but your chances of getting it right diminish. And not only that: you are also likely to be less proactive in your job as a manager. That means that you will take fewer initiatives and that your solutions to problems will probably be less of a novelty than an obvious response.

Now, to close the circle, you may be wondering where to find the sources from which to obtain the required knowledge. I would talk about four complementary sources:

1. Education
   Let us remember that 'the professional education of the decision maker' was placed by the managers of our survey in the second last position among the factors that favour the right decision-making. I would say that academic education is a convenient background but not essential to achieve the required knowledge. There are plenty of cases of people known to be rational and efficient managers with no business education. Education gives you the theoretical framework that you can leverage to better interiorize the practical knowledge of your career, and that's it. Moreover, I do not think that if you studied at, say, Stanford or Harvard, you are more prepared to acquire the necessary knowledge than if you obtained your degree at, say, Rutgers, Jönköping or Nanyang. Status does not give you the keys to knowledge.

2. Experience
   In contrast to the 'explicit knowledge' that academic education provides you with, you have the 'tacit knowledge' that experience gives. Tacit knowledge can be defined as the intelligence that a person, also a manager,

has acquired through personal and professional experience. It is made up of a set of skills or abilities that you have, although you cannot easily explain; you just know what to do and/or how to do it. You can perform many tasks, including decision-making, thanks to those vague, hard-to-document skills.

Polanyi's paradox[84] states that human knowledge capacities are far beyond our explicit understanding. Polanyi uses this sentence, "We can know more than we can say" to illustrate our limitations in explaining the learning process of the human mind. Furthermore, we are not sure how that implicit learning[85] operates. I would guess that the more and more diverse experiences are, the broader and more useful will be the tacit knowledge that a manager can acquire. Similarly, the more active the attitude in exchanging experiences, the more intense will be the exercise of tacit knowledge. Therefore, it seems advisable to be exposed to a wide range of contexts, positions, perspectives and groups. The capacity for apprehension, fundamental for converting information into knowledge, emerges again as a critical factor.

Although, by definition, it is not possible to take control of tacit knowledge, managers must always remain alert to the conditions that I determined a few paragraphs ago for reliable knowledge: it must be continuous, close to the origin and contrasted (the three Cs). Tacit knowledge could become counterproductive or unreliable more easily than explicit knowledge.

3. Information
Everybody agrees that information is a basic source of knowledge. In fact, it is a stage prior to knowledge.

You have scattered data and events, and through a taxonomic process you convert them into understandable information, which, duly analysed, provides you with pieces of knowledge. As part of the organization's resources, you must have an in-depth knowledge of the information support systems of your company, not only because you will need to use them daily, but also because you must take into account the information available to your associates when estimating their contribution to a decision to be made.

In addition to information from your organization's decision support system, you should have reasonable knowledge of other sources, external and internal, available for ad-hoc purposes. They can be general or specialized, with a theoretical or practical bias, national or international, focused on data, news or reports, etc. You may even want to open a budget account to purchase key information that you are likely to need at any time. It is also advisable to develop in your team the ability to search for information that may require a decision or a project. And do not be mistaken: the internet is an inexhaustible source of information, but the most valuable information is not on the internet.

4. Borrowed Expertise
You may have heard of the 'weak ties theory.'[86] According to this, a social network (in the general sense; do not think exclusively of Instagram and similar) is made up of strong and weak ties. Against apparent logic, the weak ties add more value than the strong ones, which are really intense but closed to a small group of people: a community. The expansion of a network is achieved through its weak ties because they can connect different communities.

Weak ties theory can be applied to management, as it enables managers to build a network of trust and expertise based on it.

The complexity of the business context, the multiplicity of stakeholder, and the intensity of competition, added to the natural difficulty of decision-making, make it almost impossible to meet the knowledge requirements of some decisions. When the formula Education + Experience + Information is not enough to obtain the required knowledge, you may want to access the experience of some actors who are normally outside your perimeter of action to fill the knowledge gaps that you may still have at any given time. Sometimes you may simply want to save resources and time searching for hard-to-find or hard-to-interpret information so that the resource of external experience becomes a great option again. Building that network of trust and expertise will definitely help increase your chances of making the right decisions.

Let me finish this section how it started: you better not make any decision until you have acquired the necessary knowledge. You need to assess what level of knowledge is good for you in each case. I would suggest you do not give up until you have been able to assess the various trends influencing the decision, the potential risks to be faced, the potential reactions of stakeholders, and the resources and capabilities required to implement the decision. I'll give you a mnemonic acronym: WYSKBAD. It means "What you should know before any decision." Mastering the WYSKBAD is one of the greatest merits that a decision maker can present. Remember that other acronym proposed by Professor Kahneman: WYSIATI (what you see is all there is) that we discussed in section 4.10. Some managers tend to think that what they know is all they need to know. That is a position of failure. The position of success implies considering WYSIATI to embrace WYSKBAD. Good managers understand that they must gather information about the relevant knowledge they still lack on an issue about which a decision needs to be made. A manager's competence should be measured by that ability to identify the critical pieces of information necessary to obtain the required knowledge. Managerial experience must be driven to that goal and so must executive education. The difference between a junior manager and an experienced one can be seen in the ability to point out the knowledge they need (WYSKBAD –no more, no less) to make the right decision.

7.3 A HUMBLE MANAGER

Is there such a thing as a humble manager? Worse yet: can there be a humble leader? If so, we would be accepting that humility and leadership can walk together. It seems counterintuitive, right? It is thought that a manager, if they want to become a typical leader, must show self-confidence, determination, authority, efficiency, and a certain degree of fearlessness and daring. Is all that consistent with humility? Could managers be determined and humble at the same time? Yes, of course they can. Being aware of the benefits of humility at decision-making, you would also figure out the way.

So many mistakes have been made due to the arrogance and stubbornness of managers. They enjoy the power position they feel before a decision, that unique moment in which they choose the course of action to follow. Managers make a decision, and others will be affected by it. That is power, isn't it? What do they want values such as humility for? They prefer nothing to spoil the glorious moments during which they can feel like superior beings, beings that can influence the destiny of others.

You are likely a manager affected by so-called 'blind spot bias.' Don't get me wrong, it's nothing personal. Statistically, any of us can be affected. Also by the overconfidence effect, the confirmation bias or the availability-misweighing tendency. So you can tend to disdain the possible risks of any decision, or neglect to study the factors you should take into account, or reject the qualified opinions of your colleagues, or ignore any evidence that may contradict your initial idea. You do this because you tend to fool yourself by overinflating your strengths and underestimating your weaknesses; because you trust your own mind above any other possible resource and consider yourself a better decision maker than the rest; because you do not think that cognitive biases are distorting the way you assess and evaluate a problem or situation and the possible options to face it.

Instead, you can apply humility to your decisions. A humble manager shows great benefits in their activities within an organization. This book is about decision-making, so I have reflected on the consequences of humility when making decisions and have discovered quite a few positive effects. Let's see – a humble attitude as a manager will let you:

1. Not rush to make a decision. Nobody expects you to respond at lighting speed. If you make a hasty decision the only thing you prove is that you are an impulsive manager. And your chances of being right will be less than if you allow your mind the time to choose a better option. Unless it's such an obvious topic that you do not really need time to make up your mind, a good answer would be "let me think" or even better "let's think about it."

2. Appreciate the opinions and perspectives of other people. Opening the decision to your colleagues or associates is not at all a sign of weakness but of intelligence. Keeping the reflection to yourself does not mean that you are so brilliant that you do not need anyone, but rather that you do not understand the complexity of the subject and all its possible implications.

3. Be receptive to ideas contrary to your own; do not try to reinforce your opinions by paying attention just to the information that tends to confirm them.

4. Admit your weaknesses and limitations. By behaving humbly, you will usually tend toward a fair evaluation of your own abilities, acknowledge that you are not a super-hero capable of any feats, and welcome the contribution of others whose experience and skills can supplement your own. Admit that "all you see is NOT all there is."

5. Also admit that your values, beliefs and preconceptions may become a restriction to choosing the right decision; try to neutralize them by establishing sound patterns of action.

6. Understand that the values and purpose of your organization must be at all times and by all means above your own values and your own ideas about what the purpose of your company should be.

7. Take into account and give due relevance to the possible reaction of all the parts potentially affected by the decision. Consequently, think about and anticipate the effect of these possible reactions.

8. Do not underestimate the risks that the decision may incur, nor believe that in any situation you will be able to overcome them without major problems.

9. Be realistic when making plans and forecasts.

10. Agree that the short term is not the most adequate perspective when it comes to decisions of the utmost importance. Humble managers are not so concerned with the immediate results of their decisions; they do not need to touch the sky at any time or show others how sharp-witted they are.

11. Acknowledge the need for continuous training that enables you to be updated on the contextual situation the economic, social and technological trends and the evolution of the key elements that impact your industry and markets.

12. Be prone to accepting that you need a method that helps you realize a fair evaluation of the problem or situation and enhance your chances of being right when making your decision.

13. Internalize learning from mistakes and consider them a fertile part of the experience that can be used for future decisions.

14. Admit you are not ready yet to make the decision if you have not acquired the required knowledge and, in certain cases, express your difficulties in making a choice due to personal or environmental causes, such as possible conflicts of interest or too much noise and pressure around.

After reviewing the long list of benefits of humility for a manager, you may be wondering about the possible downsides. You may wonder, for example, if being humble can make you an indecisive manager or if it can be understood as having given up your responsibilities. Nothing could be more untrue. Being humble means that you give your work a relevance above your personal position and are willing to admit the limitations of a single person when it comes to making an important decision.

Let me bring in here a text from a paper by Antonio Argandoña,[87] which seems quite relevant on this point: "Neither should humility be confused with lack of strength, passivity, pusillanimity or hiding behind a cloak of anonymity or shrinking responsibilities, nor with self-deprecation or lack of self-esteem or self-confidence. Nor, of course, with lack of will or ambition: the humble person must be ambitious in the search and humble in the attainment."

I would like to finish this section with a strong conclusion: A humble manager tends to make far fewer mistakes than an arrogant one. History is full of cases where managers jeopardize their companies due to ego, arrogance or quick profits. In most of them, humility would have prevented that from happening.

7.4 SLOW MANAGEMENT

If you were a surgeon, you would have to make quick decisions to increase your patients' chances of survival. If you were a police officer, you would also have to respond quickly if you want to arrest the perpetrators. If you were a mechanic, you would have to hurry to repair the broken machine because the production line is stopped. If you were a firefighter, you would have to rapidly know how to put out the fire to prevent the building from collapsing. There are many situations where time is of the essence. However, there are others where time pressure only causes unnecessary inconvenience.

We are talking about management here. You do not see too many situations in regular organizations like the ones in the previous paragraph. Of course, there are many operations that must be carried out in due time. If your company has to pay the annual bonus on February 1, the calculations must be done before this date. If you have to teach in a training course, you better prepare the class and material in time. If a link on the online process is broken, you will make it fixed as soon as possible at the risk of losing sales.

These are mainly operational acts, though, that demand technical know-how rather than management expertise. As we have seen from the survey, managers agree that their role concerns complex stuff with multiple issues going on and different stakeholders affected.

Of course, the decision-making process cannot expand forever. There must be a deadline for decisions. But this does not necessarily mean that the deadlines should be explicit and far less rigid. Between mature and responsible professionals, there will not be much difference in time expectations. The problem is that sometimes the deadlines are set in a capricious way, with no other purpose than to put pressure and ensure theoretical effectiveness. Thus, the coordination and follow-up processes, which should focus on variables such as functionality, customer service or creativity, tend to drift toward monitoring deviations from deadlines.

In Q12 of our survey, "The availability of enough time to carry out an adequate analysis" factor ranked 14th among the 24 elements that managers consider important to make good decisions. In Q14, the "Stress, limited time available" factor ranked 11th among the 16 elements that managers consider a reason for the management error they gave as an example in the survey. Although it does not seem to be one of the critical causes of management errors, a certain influence of 'time' is confirmed even above factors such as the organizational chart or financials, for example.

As we saw in section 4.10 when reviewing the study 'Israeli Judge's Lunch,' time pressure became a bias that strongly conditioned the judges' probation decisions. Decisions benefit from having enough time to analyse the critical factors affecting a situation and the possible options available. And the quality of the decisions suffers due to the lack of sufficient time, as the previous case proved.

Missing an opportunity because you did not make up your mind quickly enough can happen once in a lifetime; making a mistake because you decide too hastily can happen all the time. So how can time help you make better decisions? Here's a list of solid arguments:

a) Time allows you to prevent falling into the trap of heuristics

b) Time allows you to better understand the problem or situation

c) Time allows you to assess the objective or objectives the decision must meet

d) Time allows you to classify the decision to make and, as a result, decide which method you are going to apply

e) Time allows you to identify all the elements involved in the situation and listed in point six of section 7.1

f) Time allows you to locate the parties potentially affected by the decision and their possible reaction to it

g) Time allows you to obtain the collaboration of people with knowledge on the subject of the decision to be made

h) Time allows you to think and even have second thoughts on the matter at stake

i) Time allows you to more fairly evaluate the different alternatives

j) Time allows you to engineer or find creative solutions to the problem

k) And time allows you to imagine the process of implementation of the decision made

The bottom line is what we can call 'slow management,' which allows managers to act neutrally when faced with a decision and, in this way, be both more effective and more efficient.

You can show some doubts about it if you understand that some decisions must be made timely to avoid an emergency situation. Just think that when you take a quick but incorrect decision, you will have to deal with the consequences of a poor result later on and will probably have to make a series of corrections that will result in a waste of time, energy and probably also money. I can show you a personal example.

When I was appointed to take over the online operations of the bank I worked for, I was eager to sell the first online products. I proposed a one-year deposit at a good interest rate plus a gift for the bank's new clients. The gift was a metal statuette picturing an activity related to the customers we were trying to appeal to, primarily liberal professionals. I remember we used a golfer statuette in the advertisements. In short, I did not spend time preparing the launch product. I made the decision based on my eagerness and intuition, and the result was a really disappointing product sale. So we decided to start over. We – now in the plural – carried out the analysis that I had failed to do the first time. After studying the motivations of our potential clients, verifying the bank's product structure and listening to the bank's head of product design (that was critical), we came up with a four-month deposit that became our first big hit. The rush to quickly launch a product online turned out to be a really bad practice. It wasted precious time and got us into trouble with our bosses. Luckily, we learned from it and from then on devoted the time required to develop our products.

One final consideration on the relationship between timing and decision-making. The schedule is not neutral either in terms of the quality of the decisions. Due to what some call 'decision fatigue,' it is not advised to take important decisions when you are tired. So you better try to make those in the morning. As Amantha Imber suggests:[88]

"When management teams meet, one of the reasons is usually to make decisions ... While a considerable amount of work goes into scheduling those meetings by diligent and patient executive assistants, the effort is concentrated around finding a window of time when everyone is available ... However, rather than simply focus on availability, people need to shift their attention to cognitive science to get the most out of their meetings ... Essentially, every single decision we make over the course of the day eats away at our decision-making 'battery,' whereby at the end of the day, our battery is running on empty. And the implication of this decision fatigue is that when making decisions, we will take the easy way out ... The vast majority of meetings are scheduled at completely random times during the day ... Worse still, some critical meetings are regularly scheduled for the afternoon or evening." According to Imber, the earlier you call a meeting where you plan to make decisions, the better the decision tends to be. It seems like an interesting tip worth keeping in mind.

7.5 THE VALUE OF COLLABORATION

In my MBA at IMD Business School, I had the opportunity to play a survival game that turned out to be an amazing experience. We were supposed to be in an extreme situation at an inhospitable place and had a set of instruments from which we could choose a few (my dubious memory tells me six) to stay safe. First, I had to do the exercise on my own, then the working groups came together to get a group solution and finally the class gathered to make the final decision. When I worked on my own, my solution gave me little chance of survival. When the group came together, we seemed to have made more qualified decisions that led us to a considerably higher probability of survival. And when the whole class got together, the different groups shared their thoughts, after which we came up with the definitive selection of the instruments. And we finally had a very high chance of surviving.

The conclusions were crystal clear to me and even more so when I realized that no one in my group had individually scored higher than the group as a whole, and no group had scored higher than the entire class. That survival game became one of the main learning experiences of the MBA, and I have kept its conclusions very vividly in my mind all these years. It demonstrated that collaborative management had the ability to sweep away the drawbacks of individual performance, provide the appropriate doses of neutrality before personal prejudices or limitations and enhance the value of knowledge in decision-making.

We could define 'collaborative management' as a way of acting and deciding together as a group of people that pursue a common purpose. The group may be made up of a team or department plus advisors, collaborators, peers, key providers and, in fact, anyone willing to participate in the decision-making process. There are two main reasons for implementing collaborative management: the lack of knowledge of individuals and their personal biases. On one hand, it is entirely impossible for a person to have all the knowledge required to make decisions due to the multiple factors influencing the decision and the complexity of a scenario crossed by numberless interrelations. On the other, the tricks of the mind that distort memories and lead to wrong conclusions may prevent correct assessments and decisions from being made. The intersection of both causes is the repeatedly mentioned 'availability-misweighing tendency' bias. It means that some managers do not even know what they do not know (unconscious incompetence). Those who know what they do not know (conscious incompetence) will be those more prone to collaborative management.

When a decision is exclusively individual, a manager's beliefs and past experiences play a key role and can distort their judgment. That is a personal process that a group overlooks through collective interaction. Collaborative decision-making will tend to dilute individual biases when they arise in discussion or in the decision process. People suffer from personal biases, as we have learned throughout the book. It is unlikely that a group suffers from collective biases that could easily distort the conclusions of the group work. This is the reason collaborative management turns out to be much more neutral with regard to decision-making than typical individual management.

As a result of the preceding paragraphs, one of the first tasks you should face in assuming a managerial responsibility would be to secure a good team of associates and advisers. They can provide you with experience, technical knowledge, a broader perspective, different points of view, a fair assessment of risks and a guarantee of neutrality. In the Introduction of the aforementioned *Thinking, Fast and Slow*, Daniel Kahneman writes: "We are often confident even when we are wrong, and an objective observer is more likely to detect our errors than we are."

If collaborators are able to set up and expose their own judgment, they can become key tools for neutrality at decision-making. Many managers – especially the humble kind – admit that they are not the most intelligent person in the organization, not even on their team often enough. But provided you get to put together a dynamic and motivated group that enjoys a sense of unity, and encourage members to express themselves freely, respecting differences and trying to build on each contribution, you do not need to be the smartest or even the most experienced in the group. This is the beauty of collaborative management and, specifically, of collaborative decision-making.

How do you implement collaborative management in your decisions? First, as stated above, you must build a reliable team with different skills and experiences; the more diverse, the more neutral in making decisions. Next, you need to ensure that the members of your team or decision group have a clear understanding of the purposes and values of your organization and also of your unit within that organization. You will have to inject trust into the group as soon as possible, which you will get through a combination of honesty, fairness, transparency and a sense of common interest. Yes, you must be an example of honest behaviour and demand total honesty from each member of the group; you must make a fair evaluation of opinions and contributions regardless of who their author is; you must provide for the group all the information available on the decision to be taken; and you have to be sure that the whole group shares a common objective that will be above any individual interest.

I have drawn the following chart to express this process graphically:

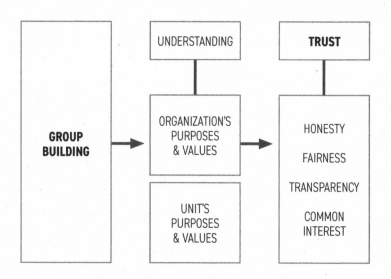

FIGURE 12: COLLABORATIVE DECISION-MAKING

Now you are ready to make your decisions in collaborative mode whenever you think you need it. You could do this by consensus or using some voting system. If you believe that there may be any halo effect (section 4.10), HiPPO effect (section 5.3) or any of this kind acting on the group, you can do so anonymously.

7.6 A SYNTHETIC FORMULA FOR DECISION EASING

In section 6.3, I talked about a start-up project to produce vegetable-based dough to be baked at home and turned into tasty, sugar-free snacks. The founders did the right thing to get expert opinions, and this was what they collected. The first expert recommended a classic approach and addressing mainly small food shops; another claimed selling online would be the best safe option; a third did not hesitate to target supermarket chains. Meanwhile, the founders received a proposal to purchase 1,000 healthy donuts a day for one school with the added prospect of expanding the order to other schools. One of the partners argued that care homes could be an even better target. The funny thing is that nobody developed any analysis, that everybody gave their opinion on a heuristics basis, with the sole input being each individual experience.

Therefore, the queries did not sort out which segment and channel were the most suitable for the project. The founders had information from their analysis and experience from the opinions of experts, but they still did not feel confident enough to make a decision. The solution came after defining a clear objective and precise selection criteria. The objective was to achieve the break-even point in two years and reach €4 million in sales in the third year. The decision criteria were the volume of investment, the chances of scalability and access to the market. By using an easy calculation method, they were able to find a synthetic number that helped them move forward with the project.

On some occasions, no matter how much knowledge you have acquired on a subject, you may need a synthetic formula that clears your mind and makes the decision easier and free of possible prejudices. Synthesis can be defined as the combination of the parts of an analysis to facilitate deductive reasoning. It is a basic factor of neutrality. When it comes to decision-making, some solutions have been around for a long time. We have, for example, Multiple Criteria Decision-making (MCDM). You can find in any mathematical source how it works, even in Wikipedia. I like it because it is not too complicated, and it allows you to apply knowledge in a systematic way. Criteria tend to defuse prejudice and therefore prove to be a straight source of neutrality. I can remind you how MCDM works through an imaginary example.

So, imagine your company wants to shorten the average procurement time by 20% before 12 months without increasing costs. You have come up with four possible alternatives:

a) Renegotiate the current procurement service contracts
b) Change of suppliers, giving preference to local companies
c) Implementation of a tracking module in the procurement application
d) In-house development of an entirely new application

The first thing to do would be to establish the decision criteria, give each one a weight and determine if their effect is direct or inverse; that is, if their application favours or goes against the value of the alternatives. The criteria in the case would be the following:

CRITERIA	WEIGHT	EFFECT
1. Risk of supply discontinuity	25%	Inverse
2. Potential reduction in provisioning time	35%	Direct
3. Cost of the solution	25%	Inverse
4. Reduction of supplier dependency	15%	Direct

Some of these criteria have an implicit value of their own. The 'C2. Potential reduction in provisioning time' could be, for example, 10%, 35% or 60%. To evaluate other criteria, we will have to use an intermediate step. In our case, we must define that intermediate scale for the factors 'C1. Risk of supply discontinuity' and 'C4. Reduction of supplier dependency.'

SCALE OF C1. RISK OF SUPPLY DISCONTINUITY:

Continuity of supply is almost guaranteed	1
There is a small risk of a little discontinuity	2
There is a medium risk of a not-so-little discontinuity	3
There is a notable risk of a relevant discontinuity	4

SCALE OF C4. REDUCTION OF SUPPLIER DEPENDENCY

Not significant variation is expected	1
Small reduction of overall dependency is possible	2
An appreciable reduction could be achieved	3
A remarkable reduction of dependency is expected	4

Now, we should build this table with the data obtained from the analysis of the elements affecting the decision and which I am going to make up for the sake of the exercise. The criteria are identified as C1, C2, C3 and C4 following the 'criteria table' on the previous page.

	CRITERIA			
ALTERNATIVES	C1	C2	C3	C4
A. Renegotiate contracts	2	20%	50	1
B. Change of suppliers	4	25%	250	3
C. Implementation of a tracking module	1	15%	125	2
D. Development of a new application	2	25%	400	2

Next, we must get the Maximum Value (MaxV) for the criteria with direct effect and the Minimum Value (MinV) for the criteria with inverse effect. These would be:

MinV C1: 1   MaxV C2: 25%   MinV C3: 50   MaxV C4: 4

And apply the homogenization formula which would be MinV / V for the inverse effect criteria and V/MaxV for the direct effect criteria, where V is the value of each criterion for each alternative. By doing this, we would get the following numbers:

ALTERNATIVES	C1	C2	C3	C4
A. Renegotiate contracts	0.50	0.80	1.00	0.25
B. Change of suppliers	0.25	1.00	0.20	0.75
C. Implementation of a tracking module	1.00	0.60	0.40	0.50
D. Development of a new application	0.50	1.00	0.13	0.50

We can see that, for instance, Alternative C gets the highest value in C1, because it implies no risk of supply discontinuity whereas Alternative A gets the lowest value in C4, because it has no effect on the supplier dependency criterion. Finally, we apply the weight of each criterion to obtain the final evaluation table by adding the four values:

ALTERNATIVES	C1	C2	C3	C4	TOTAL
A. Renegotiate contracts	0.13	0.28	0.25	0.04	0.70
B. Change of suppliers	0.06	0.35	0.05	0.11	0.57
C. Implementation of a tracking module	0.25	0.21	0.08	0.10	0.64
D. Development of a new application	0.13	0.35	0.03	0.08	0.59

According to the MCDM method, the renegotiation of the current procurement contracts would be the correct decision to make; on the contrary, the change of suppliers would be the least recommendable option. In addition to the benefit of obtaining a synthetic value as a conclusion of the whole analysis, the method makes you rethink the whole thing and compare factors among the identified alternatives. It also allows you to play with the evaluation by changing the values to the criteria according to possible different assessments or interpretations. Once you have applied a criteria-based method, the decision will become easier for you and also more neutral.

Although, as I said, I like MCDM, I am not sure that some managers want to go through such a process or that the operative dynamics of many organizations make it convenient. But you still need a synthetic formula for those decisions that are less straightforward. You may want something simpler and more intuitive. I suggest this other easy formula that synthesizes the effect of three key aspects for any decision, as we have seen throughout the book:

- Your decision must increase the chances of meeting the objective; that is your goal. There will be alternatives whose implementation brings you closer to the objective more than others. Establishing a measurement criteria will help you assess how much.
- As long as each alternative is successfully implemented, it will have greater or lesser potential to generate benefits. Each alternative may meet the objective to a different extent than the others. That benefit potential would be another element of the formula. For a fair evaluation, you will first need to establish criteria.

- Whether the alternative fails once implemented or does work out, you will incur risks, the first of which are the expenses involved in its deployment. Again, you will have to set some criteria to include risk in the equation.

Let me use the same example as in the MCDM exercise to illustrate how PBR would work. First, the scales of each element must be defined:

SCALE OF 'P: PROBABILITY OF MEETING THE OBJECTIVE':

Difficult. Estimate of a maximum probability of 25%	1
There is a certain possibility. Between 25 and 50%	2
Quite probable. Between 50 and 75%	3
Most likely. Between 75 and 100%	4

SCALE OF 'B: BENEFITS POTENTIAL':

Not much reduction in time or supplier dependency	1
Some possible extra time reduction with no impact on dependency	2
Some possible extra reduction in time and dependency	3
Expectations of further time and dependency reduction	4

SCALE OF 'R: RISK LEVEL' (INVERSE EFFECT):

Supply continuity guaranteed and small expense to incur	1
Small risk of supply discontinuity and some minor expenses	2
Appreciable risk of discontinuity and significant expense	3
High risk of discontinuity with minor expense	4
High risk of discontinuity with significant expense	5

Note that you can handle the scales according to your own criteria and using as many values and levels as you consider appropriate.

Now we should apply the above criteria to the alternatives available and calculate the final value through the formula: P x B / R. This could look like in this table:

ALTERNATIVES	P	B	R	TOTAL
A. Renegotiate contracts	2	2	1	4.00
B. Change of suppliers	3	3	4	2.25
C. Implementation of a tracking module	2	1	1	2.00
D. Development of a new application	3	2	3	3.00

According to the PBR formula, we should choose the renegotiation of current contracts as the best decision to make. In this fictitious case, it agrees with the MCDM recommendation, although that does not always happen in real life.

I was the only participant in the exercise. If it were a real case, I would recommend involving other people to make it collaborative. You will raise the degree of neutrality of the analysis, and the chances of being right would increase.

As a final comment on this section, I do not think the method you use to synthesize your decision-making is that important. The important thing is the work of acquiring the knowledge to be able to set criteria, picture what the implementation of each alternative would be like and apply the criteria to those alternatives you have previously identified. For those decisions where the complexity is high and the factors involved are many, you may want to use a synthetic formula that clears the way and brings new doses of neutrality. You could use MCDM, PBR, both or whatever you figure out. This is my final message about it.

7.7 PRACTICE WITH HISTORY

Management literature is only useful when it is put into practice. The functionality of a theory or a set of axioms cannot be assured unless they are applied to real cases. I propose that you review the content of this in Chapter 7, take it to June 5, 1944, the eve of D-Day, and apply its recommendations to the Normandy landings in World War II. This would be the exercise: what would you have done on that historic day? Try to free yourself from any bias on what you already know happened and also on the prevailing valuation of the landing decision. Try to place yourself in that moment and scenario and be able to make a neutral analysis and decision.

You have been appointed commander of Operation Overlord. More than 150,000 soldiers, 5,000 ships and 11,000 aircraft were deployed off the Normandy coast. The objective was to land forces and equipment, break through the defences built by the German army, and turn around the situation on the French front. Your work starts here.

You should figure out some key questions such as ...

- The ultimate purpose of the operation. The objectives defined by the Allies and the particular objectives that each country involved might have; also, the possible personal objectives of the chief commander and some other relevant person, such as the British prime minister at that time.

- The context of the operation, especially the complete panorama of the war at that time: main positions, resources and means of each party, latest evolution of the conflict, foreseeable developments.
- Time: was this the right time to make the decision to invade or was it possible to wait to see how things evolved elsewhere?
- Would you have thought of any decision criteria before issuing the invasion orders? What would those criteria be? Would the weather forecasts be your main criterion?
- Would you be pushed around by the incredible stress of the situation, or would you manage to stay calm and make a fair assessment of the factors?
- What was your knowledge of the enormous risks involved in the operation and how to overcome them? What about the chances of success of the forces under your command? What was your knowledge of the opposing German forces? Was the information received sufficiently verified?
- Aside from the obvious alternatives of invading or retreating, what other options could you handle? Could you put off the operation for a few days or weeks? Could you move the troops across a larger landing area? Could you prolong the air strikes to facilitate ground movements? Was there any other possibility beyond the obvious?
- Would you take into consideration the possible social impact of the action? In what terms?

- Would you take into account the opinions and assessments of other military or political authorities? With whom would you like to share the decision to be made? Would you try to make the decision in a collaborative way?

Do your research, talk to whoever you consider appropriate and try to answer the previous questions and all those that you think are necessary to make a decision. Finally, I propose that you reflect on the real end result of the operation and to judge whether it deserves to be remembered as a glorious event or as an unnecessary sacrifice of lives.

I just hope that you never have to face a decision as tragic as Eisenhower's regarding the Normandy landing. It is by no means easy to put yourself in his shoes so many years later. That was just a game. You will find real-life cases that require a decision to be made as soon as you close the book.

DECISION-ORIENTED ORGANIZATIONS

A decision, even when made collaboratively, ends up being a personal move. Decision-making theories focus on the action to be taken by the decision maker. The content of this book is directed primarily at women and men who are in a position to make decisions relevant to their organizations, be they large corporations, medium-sized companies, public institutions or even governments. Organizations must play a role in the quality of the decisions made within them. They have a lot to do to facilitate decision-making and the proper implementation of the decisions made.

Organizations are established according to a series of generally admitted principles: strong economic fundamentals, cost efficiency, product and service quality, brand differentiation, competitive pricing, customer segmentation, staff motivation, etc. Their main purposes tend to be to reach solid market position, do sound business and last a long time. There is no other way to achieve those objectives than by making the right decisions throughout the organization. This is the prominent factor. Now think about it: is your organization making it easier or harder for your managers and executives to take the right choices every time?

As a norm, organizations trust their executives and managers. They establish a salary according to the relevance of the decisions they must make. The more critical the decisions, the higher the salary. And the better the outcome, the bigger the bonus. However, a good outcome is not always due to a right decision. The thing is that most organizations are goal oriented. As Jonathan Baron stated,[89] "Goals are criteria by which we evaluate states of affairs, more analogous to the scoring criteria used by judges of figure-skating competitions than to the hoop in a basketball game." The question of "what does the most good" then becomes the question of "what achieves our goals best, on the whole." The implementation of organizations oriented toward *what does the most good* could be a great step forward, more so if we remember Gary Klein's words: "With an ill-defined goal, you are never sure if the decision was right." You need to know if the decision was good or bad, regardless of whether it met the goal or not.

There has been something of a consensus in recent years that agile organizations are the right model to promote sound decision-making. I picked a McKinsey paper[90] as an example that says: "The ultimate solution for many organizations looking to untangle their decision-making is to become flatter and more agile, with decision authority and account-ability going hand-in-hand ... agile organization models get decision-making into the right hands, are faster in reacting to (or anticipating) shifts in the business environment and often become magnets for top talent, who prefer working at com-panies with fewer layers of management and greater empow-erment." To be honest, although some companies operate along the lines of this concept, I see agile organizations as a wish rather than a reality. I mean, most managers and exec-utives would like their organizations to operate by following the principles that inspire that *agile concept*. And I agree that *agile principles* would make decisions more fluid and probably better, too. But transforming an enduring corporation into a purely agile organization would be a daunting challenge.

Beyond any catchword that tries to penetrate the foggy surroundings of companies, it would be truly helpful to iden-tify the concrete actions that any organization should take to help its managers make the best possible decisions. I propose the following four sets of measures:

1. The Cascade of Purposes and Objectives
   An organization must ensure that its essential purposes, its reasons for existence, its long-term aspirations, preside

over any relevant decisions of its executives and managers. Any strategic or operational plan must start from those purposes. And the establishment of the objectives in the organization must also come from those major purposes that must be recognizable by all staff.

The objectives should not be something to be negotiated between the planning division and the rest of the organization's units. They must get out of those purposes and descend into a kind of waterfall, where any objective comes from the higher objectives. The organization must ensure that goal setting makes sense, which is the best way to enforce consistency of decisions.

At the end of the year, the divisions and departments of an organization often reflect on the annual performance, check the achievement of the objectives and think about the goals for the year to come. And then their objectives may not be related to those of the rest of the organization, which is not appropriate because they will guide their actions for at least a few months. Departments seem to need a goal to look to that allows them to create the illusion of usefulness, regardless of whether or not those goals are connected to the whole organization's purpose.

The quality of the objectives is another realm to question. Goals should not just be net profit on a balance sheet, or numbers that show the rise in good variables and decline in bad variables, or how the stock price has performed last year. Just as a person is much more than a body whose health can be measured by a blood test in a certain moment, an organization is much more than the budget department and all its calculations in spreadsheets or fancy support systems. The objectives should be more qualitative than quantitative and should follow the evolution over the years of how well a strategy is working, how well projects are being managed, how customers are more or less satisfied, how products are more or less competitive, how staff are more or less committed to the organization, etc. By changing that, decisions will be better and so the results of the organization in the long run.

At this point, I would like to ask a question: Do you know of an organization that includes the "good decision ratio" objective among its goals? I do not. It should be the most important variable to monitor, shouldn't it? The organization would discuss what must be considered a good decision, the ways to qualify the decisions taken, the terms of the follow-up process and the learning conclusions to be drawn. Decisions should be an important part of the objectives of any organization. In this way, the first stone for better management would be laid.

2. New People Strategy

How do we define a strategy that helps people in the organization make better decisions? If your organization has not thought about it, it may be necessary to make some profound changes to the way it handles personnel issues. First, you need to be concerned about hiring decision-oriented people; that is, people primarily focused on making the right decisions. Throughout the book, I have been handling the concept of an ideal decision maker as one who is aware of the prominent role of knowledge, reflective rather than impulsive, who promotes the collaborative decisions, and with humility as an important element of their character. In this regard, I fully agree with Jeff Hyman when he wrote in *Forbes*:[91] "We tend to be impressed by charismatic candidates with powerful personalities and a commanding presence. My advice: dig deeper. Your gut reaction is often wrong. Search for quiet confidence, humility and a focus on others." The profile as a decision maker must definitively be one of the criteria for hiring people.

Aside from the recruitment policies, organizations should refine its organizational chart, its reward system, its training programmes and its working conditions to enhance the decision flow. An organizational chart draws the hierarchical dependences and outlines the functions of each position. To optimize decisions, it must also define the decision capabilities of each manager or senior executive, who can decide what and who must collaborate with whom. These decision criteria should consider the level of relevance of the decision, the potential risks involved and the degree of uncertainty assumed.

The reward system should be based on the quality of the decisions and their long-term effects rather than their short-term results. This would require deep reflection to choose the most appropriate concepts and design a fair form of evaluation. You should also take into account the ongoing track record of each manager rather than any value at a specific time. There is an obvious connection between the reward system and the objectives and goals setting I referred to in the previous point.

The training policy must be completely turned around. The typical KPI for the training department are usually the number of courses and attendees, the ratio hours per employee, perhaps the level of satisfaction and so on. The programs are normally designed by the training department itself at the discretion of its managers. Instead, the training programme should be a consequence of the organization's purposes and objectives and designed with the specific intention of contributing to the achievement of those purposes. A course or seminar can no longer be a sequence of hours on isolated topics without continuation in time. Each course must have its effect on the knowledge and performance of the attendees on an ongoing basis. Training must represent a continuous monitoring and evaluation of the existing capacities – decision-making among them – within the organization.

Something else on training: with decision-making the principal axe of management, training programmes should include decision-making as one of their main topics. We have been looking at the set of things that enables managers to become better decision makers. Organizations, for example, must train their managers on how to distinguish between different types of decisions, how to deal with cognitive biases, how to practice critical thinking, how to apply collaborative decision-making, or how to acquire the appropriate knowledge on a specific issue.

Regarding promotion, the organization should include the manager's profile as a decision maker among the selection criteria in a fair attempt to avoid the Peter Principle of incompetence, as I already pointed out in section 4.3. A suitable manager in a given position will not always be an effective executive at a higher level. They could make correct ad-hoc decisions in the current position, while they will tend to be wrong if assuming higher-level responsibilities.

And finally, working conditions should prevent managers and senior executives from making important decisions under the influence of fatigue or stress. The culture of working long hours every day, far from being a sign of commitment, should be understood as a potentially harmful practice that could negatively influence the quality of decisions within the organization.

3. Knowledge Ecosystem
They are usually known as 'information systems' and are made up of dozens or hundreds of screens full of formulas and data without a single remark. Some data is there in case someone needs it at any time, and other turns into reports that feed periodic meetings and boards. Although they are called 'information systems,' in many instances they are little more than a library of figures, a circumstance that may tend to increase with the emergence of big data. To become information, each block of data must include analysis and conclusions. In addition, they should be headed by the purpose of each panel and show the type of decisions they should support.

To build a knowledge ecosystem that benefits good decisions, a typical information system, though optimized, is not enough. The organization must be willing to offer its managers and senior executives the necessary resources to make decisions based on the required knowledge. In section 7.2, we have seen the knowledge areas that managers must master, and it is their organization that has to facilitate the process of building a system containing the inputs worth collecting and maintaining. This system must include a continuously updated economic outlook, reliable reports on social, technological and environmental trends, knowledge of the industry's competitive keys, the main strategies of the competitors, the perspectives of the client's needs and motives, specific technical information for each step of the value chain, the main rules that affect the business and the core resources of the organization itself.

Creating that platform or system will be a challenge. Being able to do it well and make it useful for the decisions to be made in the organization, a victory!

Think about how your organization handles information. I bet most of the time, effort and money spent on information is tied to internal data that is manipulated and presented in every imaginable way. However, where are the main threats and opportunities for your company? Can you find them digging into its internal numbers over and over again or rather in the novelties and developments that continuously emerge from an ever-changing context? What I have been calling in the book 'required knowledge' lies mainly in the external world and the management systems installed in your organization should include the significant information detected *out there*.

This is why I am talking about an 'ecosystem.' What did I mean by that? I was not referring to the wide universe of information and knowledge systems already in place frequently brought by software companies. They develop management solutions normally focused on the internal data of organizations; and it seems fair that they wish to sell them. I do not like to talk of software here, but about a dynamic that really facilitates knowledge-based decision-making. That is why I believe that the organizations themselves are the agents that should design their solutions in this area, integrating internal and external sources of high-value information. Knowledge is an essential part of the business, its pure core, and the organization must take control of it.

An ecosystem is more than a system; it is an interconnected system, an entity where all its members depend on each other. Knowledge of the organization is the task of all staff. It must be shared openly and put at the service of the whole on a permanent basis. In addition to building a system, the organization must organize frequent meetings where the different units and managers submit their main projects, insights, findings, breakthroughs and learnings. This way of working will be transferred to decision-making and then, finally, it may be said that the organization is really based on knowledge.

4. A Decision Platform
The procurement function is important in many organizations, and that is why they have a procurement application; customer service is important in all organizations, and that is why most have a customer relationship management application; personnel administration is important for most organizations, and that is why they usually have an application to manage the relationship with employees; key performance indicators are also important in many organizations, and that is why they have a KPI application. Decision-making is absolutely critical for any organization, yet almost no organization has a decision process application.

In section 7.1, I establish the principles that managers must take into account to design – perhaps only in their mind – a method to make good decisions. I did not want to propose any specific method because, as I have said several times, each manager is their own inspiration when making decisions. This does not mean that organizations cannot assume that responsibility and try to get their managers and senior executives to follow a path that ensures that important decisions are taken with due guarantees.

As is often the case, the answer is systematization, the core of which must be an application or platform that guides managers toward a suitable method. That platform should consider the different types of decisions and be used only in the case of those relevant or complex enough to require the support of the decision system. According to the content of Chapter 7, it must contain at least the following functions:

a) Description of the situation and its context
b) Definition of the objectives to be met by the decision and the general purposes linked to them
c) Definition of the people involved in the process and their possible roles to play
d) Determination of the criteria to generate alternatives of action and choose among them
e) Identification of the information to be collected
f) Identification of possible advisers to provide the necessary knowledge for decision-making
g) Assessment of the risks that can be incurred and the means to overcome them
h) Assessment of their own resources and capabilities needed to implement each alternative
i) Evaluation of potential parties affected by the decision and anticipation of their possible reactions
j) Possible rules with a potential effect on the decision
k) The requesting of possible reports – already done or to be done – necessary to gain the required knowledge
l) Open discussion
m) Synthetic method of valuation and choice (section 7.6)
n) Approach to the communication and implementation of the chosen solution

(One might wonder: what about artificial intelligence? I would not mix things up. A decision platform is necessary to optimize decision-making in organizations. Time will tell what AI can achieve in terms of management decisions.)

Some may think that, by using a platform like the one projected above, the organization would be generating bureaucracy, but it is the other way around. Imagine the long and sometimes repetitive meetings that would be spared, the many emails that would not get sent, the laborious reports that would not get done, the amount of information that would not need to be collected. The systematization of the decision process in organizations will not only improve the outcome of most decisions but will also make the process more effective and efficient.

Some books offer conclusions, which is, to a certain extent, illogical. The reader is supposed to be the one to draw their conclusions. In fact, any section may become a conclusion, any page, any paragraph, maybe even just a single sentence. I will not finish with my conclusions but with one last comment.

Managers tend to ignore mistakes, to work as if management mistakes do not exist. But they do exist. Admitting that anyone is often wrong is the first step to becoming a better decision maker. Throughout *The Wrong Manager*, I have tried to identify and show the main reasons for management mistakes and the appropriate action patterns to greatly reduce the chances of serious mistakes in an organization. Now you can try to make some changes to your own management exercise. In that case, you may encounter some resistance from your colleagues. If that happens, you might get frustrated and want to go back to the old way of making decisions. That is why it would be so important that the changes in decision methods were implemented in the organization as a whole. In that way, those changes would inspire a new philosophy of action across its divisions and units, starting with the CEO, who has the power of transformation. If the CEO adopts the patterns of behaviour included in *The Wrong Manager*, those will descend throughout the organization, and the results will soon be noticed in many crucial respects.

Let me finally end with some words from Jeff Hyman in an aforementioned *Forbes* article: "When a leader works to harness input from everyone, it carries through the organization. As other executives and line managers emulate the leader's approach, a culture of getting the best from every team and every individual takes root." I feel it would be especially applicable to management decision-making.

APPENDIX 1.
THE SURVEY

Through this survey we will try to understand how management decisions work and the nature of management mistakes. First, you should briefly describe a real example of what you think was **a serious management error**, whether it was made in your organization or in another one, or whether it was made by yourself or by someone you may or may not know. No need to mention any names.

BRIEF DESCRIPTION OF A MANAGEMENT ERROR THAT YOU HAVE KNOWLEDGE OF

1. How would you classify the decision made in your example?
   a) A critical error:

   it had a relevant effect on the future of the organization
   b) A serious error:

   it had a relevant effect on key performance variables of the organization
   c) A controllable error:

   its consequences could be controlled without large cost or effort
   d) A restricted error:

   it affected just one part of the organization but not the whole

2. How would you classify the complexity of the decision made in your example?

   (if it is not in the list, please check the closest type):
   a) A simple decision in which the cause-effect relationships were well known.
   b) A difficult decision due to the large number of elements to take into consideration
   c) A complex decision with relevant potential influence on several stakeholders
   d) A critical decision which could jeopardize the future of the organization

3. In which area of the organization was the decision of your example made? (if it is not in the list, please check the closest area)
   a) General Strategy
   b) Finance or Investment
   c) Human Resources
   d) Production / Operations
   e) Technology
   f) Marketing and Product Design
   g) Sales and Customer Service
   h) Administration

4. How do you think the decision in your example was made?
   (check the answer that best matches your idea)
   a) As soon as the decision maker understood the situation, he/she expressed what had to be done
   b) He/she decided after a short period of reflection based on a little information
   c) He/she made the decision after a thorough analysis process
   d) He/she made the decision after a process of analysis and in agreement with his/her colleagues

5. Still regarding the decision in your example: as far as the process, check the answer that best suits your idea.
   a) The decision was a Yes / No choice
   b) The decision was made between two different alternatives
   c) Several alternatives were on the table to make the decision
   d) The decision maker came up with a solution different from the alternatives evaluated

6. As far as the management mistake you described at the beginning of the form, why do you consider it to be a poor decision?
   (you can check more than one answer):
   a) It was not the best possible option
   b) The organization was in a worse position after the decision
   c) Inadequate balance between costs and benefits
   d) The decision made the organization assume an important risk
   e) The decision was made without the required process of analysis
   f) The decision focused on the short term and ignored the long-term effects
   g) The decision was inconsistent with the objective pursued
   h) The decision made the organization lose money
   i) The decision made no sense

7. How do you think important decisions of an organization should be made? (check the answer that best matches your idea)
   a) Quickly, once the decision maker understands the situation, there is no time to waste
   b) After a short period of reflection based on one's own experience and after checking the key information
   c) After a thorough process of analysis considering all the factors involved in the situation
   d) After a thorough process of analysis and in agreement with colleagues who are competent with regard to the situation

8. How do you think most of the important decisions of an organization are actually made? (check the answer that best matches your idea)
   a) Quickly, once the decision maker understands the situation
   b) After a short period of reflection based on one's own experience and after checking the key information
   c) After a thorough process of analysis considering all the factors involved in the situation
   d) After a thorough process of analysis and in agreement with the colleagues with a competent word in the situation

9. Imagine that managers fall into two categories or profiles: the 'impulsive' ones who tend to make their decisions as soon as they understand the problem, and the 'analytical' ones who tend to decide after a thorough analysis. Check the answer that best suits your thinking on this topic.
   a) Managers tend to decide according to their profile as decision makers no matter how complex the problem can be
   b) 'Impulsive' managers always make quick decisions even when the problem is complex
   c) 'Analytical' managers always follow a thorough decision process even when the problem is simple
   d) Both impulsive and analytical managers adapt their way of deciding to the complexity of the problem to be solved

10. What do you think can be considered a good decision?
    (check the answer that best matches your idea):
    a) The best option of all the possible alternatives
    b) Any decision which provides a good result to the organization
    c) Any decision made after a thorough process of analysis and consistent
       with the objective pursued
    d) Both b) and c) look correct to me

11. An important decision in the organization must be made by:
    check 1 if you do not agree, 2 if you agree a little, 3 if you agree in most cases,
    and 4 if you do totally agree.

AN IMPORTANT DECISION MUST BE MADE BY	1	2	3	4
a) The manager in charge of the issue because the situation is their responsibility				
b) The manager in charge after reaching an agreement with his or her team to minimize the odds of error				
c) The manager in charge and his or her team so that everybody can feel responsible for the decision				
d) The manager in charge after getting sign-off from his or her boss to minimize potential conflicts				
e) The manager in charge after being sure that all the required information was taken into account				
f) The manager in charge after going through a complete and rigorous analysis				

12. How important are the following elements to making a good decision?
(check 1 if you think it is not important, 2 if you think it is somewhat important,
3 if you think it is fairly important or 4 if you think it is absolutely critical)

IMPORTANT ELEMENTS FOR A GOOD DECISION	1	2	3	4
a) The experience of the decision maker				
b) The knowledge of the decision maker				
c) The professional education of the decision maker				
d) The personality of the decision maker				
e) The mood and state of mind of the decision maker				
f) The leadership style of the decision maker				
g) The team and advisors of the decision maker				
h) The tendency of the manager to make team decisions				
i) The correct definition of the objective				
j) The alignment between personal and corporate goals				
k) The distinction between short-term and long-term effects				
l) The use of extensive information				
m) The availability of an effective information system				
n) A good financial study				
o) An accurate evaluation of the risks faced by the decision				
p) A clear organization chart and allocation of responsibilities				
q) A clear process in the organization to make decisions				

IMPORTANT ELEMENTS FOR A GOOD DECISION	1	2	3	4
r) Being able to take into consideration all the parties affected by the decision				
s) Being able to understand the context affecting the decision				
t) Being able to understand the market and industry trends affecting the decision				
u) The availability of enough time to carry out an adequate analysis				
v) The level of the operational stress in the organization				
w) The level of personal conflicts in the organization				
x) Good luck				
y) Another factor (please write)				

13. Read the following descriptions and choose whether you consider each one: 1 a good decision; 2 a poor decision; 3 depends on the circumstances.

WHAT IS A GOOD OR POOR DECISION FOR YOU	1	2	3
a) A decision made through a solid analytical process that met the required goals			
b) A decision made through a solid analytical process that had got a positive outcome but did not fully meet the required goals			
c) A decision made through a solid analytical process that did not meet the required goals			
d) A decision made after a little reflection that met the required goals			
e) A decision made after a little reflection that got a positive outcome but did not fully meet the required goals			
f) A decision made after a little reflection that did not meet the required goals			
g) An automatic or spontaneous decision that nevertheless met its required goals			
h) An automatic or spontaneous decision that got a positive outcome but did not meet the required goals			
i) An automated or spontaneous decision that did not meet the required goals			

14. Going back to the management mistake you described at the beginning of the form, which do you think were the reasons for the mistake: (check 1 if you think it was not a reason at all, 2 if you think it has a little influence, 3 if you think it had a relevant effect or 4 if you think it was the main or one of the main reasons)

POSSIBLE REASONS	1	2	3	4
a) Ineffective or not clear definition of the objective				
b) The profile of the manager who made the decision				
c) The influence of cognitive biases				
d) A poor selection of the necessary information				
e) An underestimation of the risks involved				
f) An overvaluation of the organization's capabilities				
g) To prioritize short-term over long-terms effects				
h) An inadequate consideration of some context elements				
i) Not taking into account a possible reaction from customers				
j) Not taking into account a possible reaction from competitors				
k) Misleading calculations; bad work with numbers				
l) Lack of a financial study				
m) An adequate analysis process was not followed				
n) The organization does not have a clear organization chart				
o) Stress, limited time available				
p) Bad luck				
q) If other, which one:				

15. Please select the person who made the decision in your example at the beginning of the form: (if it is not in the list, please check the closest profile)
    a) Your boss, an experienced manager
    b) Your boss, a novice manager
    c) A colleague, an experienced manager
    d) A colleague, a novice manager
    e) A top executive of the organization where you are/were working at that time
    f) A top executive of an organization you are/were not working for at that time
    g) A politician
    h) Yourself

APPENDIX 2.
LIST OF MANAGEMENT ERRORS COLLECTED IN THE SURVEY[II.]

1. Having opened a whole operation in a new market without any proper analysis which turned out badly.

2. Failing to cover the necessary knowledge about the subject before evicting a settlement of some ethnic minority people.

3. Hiring the wrong person for the job.

4. The launch of a machine similar to an ATM to be located in gas stations for the sale of supplementary and diverse services. As had been noted, the project was a total failure.

5. Hiring a sales manager with the wrong capabilities.

6. Extreme lack of top-down communication in the restructuring of an area of the company.

7. Not being transparent with the customer (in a B2B framework). The customer eventually realized that critical information was not being shared, and the result was a substantial loss of trust.

8. Retaining an executive who wanted to leave the company.

9. The treatment of risk in financial institutions during the real state bubble.

10. Lack of coordination in a negotiation that involved two countries. They signed the deal in one of the markets, which affected the pending agreements in the other.

11. The expansion of a branch network of a bank in the hottest moment of the economic cycle.

12. The purchase of a software tool that did not work out any problem or add any extra value, although it made the processes far more complicated.

13. Policy of excessive growth in the marketing of risk products without taking into account market variables.

14. Trying to expand in a foreign market based exclusively on technical advantages and without considering key factors such as legislation or taxation.

15. Investing in sales and marketing before the product was ready.

16. Avoiding paying commissions to the sales force that caused low motivation and staff resignations.

17. Underquoting on a complex but promising project.

ii. Some of the texts have been slightly modified in order to improve the wording or reduce their length. A few were not published because they were not specific cases but rather generic statements.

18. Mistakenly assuming that a project was well managed because the client showed some satisfaction.

19. Reluctance to delegate a noncritical task to ensure the quality level of the process.

20. Leading an organization through decisions made on subjective judgments, political issues and personal relationships.

21. Not assigning tasks directly to certain team members and letting them decide who did what, which ultimately led to some tasks not being completed on time or even carried out at all.

22. Poor site selection for a retail store.

23. Losing track of a project by not following its development and measuring the results of each phase.

24. Implementing a growth strategy with the main goal of increasing the size of the financial statements.

25. The sales team of a pharmaceutical distribution firm were offered low-class rental cars for three years. At the end of the period, the cars were returned to the car rental company. This resulted in poor-quality driving with physical consequences for the sales team, and financial losses for the pharmaceutical firm. Leasing a higher-end car would have resulted in safer driving, better employee valuation and the possibility of getting a bonus for reselling the vehicle.

26. Launch of a new product line with insufficient support that was not successful.

27. The president of a multinational corporation hires a highly qualified CEO without anticipating that his psychological profile would lead him to dispute the chair of the board. The president ended up firing him with the consequent compensation and reputational damage.

28. Having negotiated an important contract while ignoring its consequences in the long run.

29. Bad management of segments and markets. Refusing to enter the Portuguese market and deciding to expand to new Spanish regions, abandoning the business associated with small- and medium-sized companies to reinforce the growth of mortgages for families.

30. Presentation of a project to implement an Intellectual capital management model. The staff were not prepared for that, and the reaction was negative.

31. A new CEO was hired. He came from another company and replicated the same management model despite the great differences between the two organizations.

32. Not hiring user experience professionals and letting engineers do the job when they were neither trained nor motivated for that.

33. Considering other areas of the company as enemies and acting accordingly.

34. Deceiving and convincing myself that I could get along with the manager who hired me when I already knew he was very difficult to deal with.

35. Sticking to traditional products and thus not understanding and adapting to the evolution of our customers' preferences.

36. Establishing an internal competitor that lowered prices and irritated the customers.

37. Giving up and selling the company to a multinational corporation.

38. Third-generation family members placed in management positions despite inadequate preparation instead of employees with long history and experience in the company.

39. Two years after founding the first online foreign exchange trading company in the country, an opportunity to open an office in Asia presented itself. Knowing the person who was to run the office in Asia, a decision was quickly made to open the office without an intensive analysis. The effort never really took off due to the inability of the person as a manager, the distance and the amount of work and focus that was needed in Europe. After a few years, it was decided to shut down the operation.

40. Preventing from making an important strategic decision for fear of being wrong.

41. Human resources does not follow a manager's proposal about an employee who creates a bad environment and has a high degree of absenteeism. Things only got worse until finally the employee himself sues the company and thereby obtains a compensation higher than what would correspond to him.

42. Appointing a person as manager of an area about which they don't even know the basics.

43. Inefficiency and failure to meet the deadlines due to the lack of rigour in management procedures.

44. Misallocation of resources, starting a project that finally does not work, which generated problems in an entire area of the organization.

45. Error of assessment due to fear of change, which caused the loss of an opportunity derived from the digitization of processes.

46. Lack of long-term vision when we ran out of projects and clients and did not seek new market niches. That would require collaboration between two departments, which was considered a nuisance. This decision mistake caused a department to go from 10 to three members in one year.

47. Leave the management of the development department in the hands of a technical partner, without specific knowledge for it.

48. Maintain operations in China despite lack of profit and high uncertainties on the future of patents and prices.

49. The decision to postpone the repatriation of dividends from the Brazilian branch based on the high interest paid in the country in 2017–2018. Currency risk assessment was overly optimistic.

50. Applying economies of scale in business areas where manpower services are the core activity.

51. A greedy strategy based on rapid expansion and aggressive selling tactics. Hiring managers oblivious to corporate culture and focused on short-term results. Expansion to unknown markets already saturated, assuming high risk operations with prices lower than those of the competition. Prioritize short-term volume over credit quality. This strategy exacerbated the attitude of the managers whose prestige and compensation depended on how quickly their business areas grew.

52. The error consisted in developing a new product line and not deciding on the necessary changes in the organization to create the infrastructure to support the new line.

53. Not having correctly defined the scope of the project, causing an important rework.

54. Not accepting external funding or a financial partner.

55. A new CEO brought outdated ideas to the company. He decided to weaken our online operations and strengthen traditional channels. Today we are still trying to rebuild what he dismantled some years ago.

56. Failed distribution strategy of my company in the US.

57. When organizing an event, there was a communication error between the supplier and my department, so all the layout (tents, stages ...) had to be changed the day before the start.

58. Hiring the wrong person.

59. Trusting the team to finish a project. When I came back after a few days away, everything was a mess. We couldn't sort it out in time, so the delivery work was not satisfactory.

60. Errors in the management of shipments that resulted in noncompliance with deadlines and response times.

61. Company A, headquartered in Singapore, has regional sales rights for a particular brand of equipment in a few Southeast Asian countries. In these regional markets, Company A has used a system of distributors to manage and develop the business, with some oversight and control. In one of these countries (let's name it Market B), it was a closely related party that was assigned as the distributor (Distributor C). Over the years, Market B had not performed well, with its competitors overtaking it in organization setup, branding and marketing, sales and after-sales support. Due to the close and sensitive relationship between Company A and Distributor C, it was difficult for Company A to perform market audits, rectify issues, push directives or change distributors. This has led to continued poor performance in Market B.

62. The acting president of an association to which I belong decided to register it in a Public Registry, which was considered a good initiative. The mistake came from having unilaterally chosen two other members to act as secretary and treasurer for registration purposes, causing critical problems later on.

63. We planned to change our support software to clients. We knew that was going to be a huge process that would cause many operational problems. We tried to convince HR to reinforce the contact centre for at least one month. Instead of the number of people we demanded, we were allowed to hire just a very few, and the replacement process ended up being a nightmare, with thousands of clients really pissed off.

64. Making an organizational decision relying primarily on numbers.

65. We changed the ad agency. They convinced us to substitute our image and marketing values, which was a mistake.

66. Buy a competitor to absorb market share.

67. It is common to understand innovation processes as if they were simple renovations of equipment, cosmetic updates or aspirational stories that do not usually include the transformation of thinking and internal processes. One case in which I participated was a frozen fish company devoted to private labels that decided to develop a line of new products to market under its own brand. The company invested in the development of the brand, added new production lines, created new products, wrote a marketing plan ... did everything necessary for the implementation of the new brand, except changing the mentality and processes. After five years, two changes in the steering committee and even developing a baby food line with Disney, they failed to position their brand.

68. This situation came up as a poor-quality service from a supplier. After significant meetings with our senior executives, the CEO decided to align with his team instead of understanding that they were not delivering. He lost his job a few months later and was replaced by somebody who understood that operational excellence was key to business success.

69. A change in the commercial division, adding a new level that separated the top management from the staff that served customers.

70. Starting a new consulting company without sufficient knowledge of the industry and at the worst time of the economic cycle.

71. A project in which nobody was concerned about the team motivation, and everything was left to improvisation.

72. Not making decisions at the right moment, thinking that over time things would get better on their own.

73. Ongoing assignation of difficult tasks to people without the proper qualification and experience.

74. Even though this manager had an assigned responsibility, he continued to allow his boss to decide for him, so he was eventually dismissed.

75. Absolute focus on service management without worrying about updating the product portfolio.

76. It looks like a silly mistake, but it was quite critical. Our company partnered with a smaller one with the necessary expertise to gain a contract. In the sales process, we decided to join the references of clients and success cases. So, to check the references, the prospect called some of these clients who did not know us because they were customers of our partner's. This caused us to lose an important contract that we had almost gained.

77. Delaying the decision to abandon a business line that was consuming a lot of resources. The expected changes in the market already suggested that this would not be sustainable over time.

78. Letting a person stay longer than appropriate in a position by assuming a) he would change b) fear of him being absolutely necessary.

79. The whim of exchanging professionals between different areas of the company.

80. Not clearly explaining the goals and responsibilities of each person in a developing area.

81. A negotiation process in which my interlocutors had no autonomy to negotiate, and I was not aware until it was too late.

82. Making the wrong decision to finance a group subsidiary by guiding us through the day-to-day market and not rethinking the long-term strategy of the project.

83. We presented a project highlighting its solidarity aspect, which was misinterpreted as a paternalistic attitude toward the target community.

REFERENCES

1. Hickson, Dave J., Butler, Richard J., & Wilson, David C. (2001). *The Bradford Studies of Strategic Decision Making.* London. Taylor & Francis Group.

2. Papamichail, K.N., & Rajaram, V. (2007). A framework for assessing best practices in decision making. Manchester Business School, University of Manchester.

3. Quine, W. V., & Ulliam, J.S. (1970). *The web of belief.* New York. Random House.

4. Gigerenzer, G., & Gaissmaier, W. (2011) Heuristic Decision Making. *Annual Journal of Psychology.* 62(1):451-82.

5. Eustachewich, L. (5 January 2021). Rep. Lauren Boebert releases video of herself walking around DC with gun. *New York Post.* Retrieved from https://nypost.com/2021/01/05/rep-lauren-boebert-loads-gun-walks-around-dc-in-new-video/#.

6. Brady United. (20 February 2021). The Facts That Make Us Act. Retrieved from https://www.bradyunited.org/key-statistics.

7. Campitelli, G., & Gobet, F. (2010). Herbert Simon's decision-making approach: investigation of cognitive processes in experts. DOI-10.1037/a0021256. *Review of General Psychology.* 14(4):354-364.

8. Hoefer, R., & Green Jr., S. (2016). A rhetorical model of institutional *Decision Making*: the role of rhetoric in the formation and change of legitimacy judgments. *Academy of Management Review*. 41. 130-150. 10.5465/amr.2014.0330.

9. Miller, C. R. (1989) The rhetoric of decision science, or Herbert A. Simon *Says. Journal of Science, Technology, & Human Values*, vol. 14, no. 1, pp. 43–46. Retrieved from www.jstor.org/stable/689668.

10. Tversky, A., & Kahneman, D. (1986). Rational choice and the framing of decisions. *The Journal of Business*. 59 (4): 251–278.

11. Pugh, D. S., & Hickson, D.J. (2007). *Writers on Organizations, 6th Edition*. Management and Decision-Making in Organizations. Chapter 3. pp 95-128. Newbury Park, California. SAGE Publishing. https://www.corwin.com/sites/default/files/upm-binaries/15500_Chapter_3.pdf.

12. Tversky, A., & Kahneman, D. (1979). Prospect Theory: An Analysis of Decision under Risk. *Econometrica*, Vol. 47, No. 2 (Mar., 1979), pp. 263-291.

13. Kahneman, D. (2011). *Thinking fast and slow*. New York. Straus and Giroux Farrar.

14. Klein, Gary. (1999). *Sources of Power. How People Make Decisions*. The MIT Press.

15. Herbig, B., & Glöckner, A. (2009). Experts and decision making: first steps towards a unifying theory of decision making in novices, intermediates and experts. DOI: 10.2139/ssrn.1337449. SSRN Electronic Journal.

16. Evans, J. (2008). Dual-processing accounts of reasoning, judgment, and social cognition. *Annual Review of Psychology*. DOI: 10.1146/annurev.psych.59.103006.093629. pp. 255-278.

17. Kahneman, D., Knetsch, J.L., &Thaler, R.H. (1991). Anomalies: the endowment effect, loss aversion, and status quo bias. *Journal of Economic Perspectives*, 5(1), pp.193-206.

18. Thaler, R. H., & Sunstein, C. R. (2008). *Nudge: improving decisions about health, wealth and happiness.* Yale University Press.

19. Thaler, Richard H. (1999). Mental Accounting Matters. *Journal of Behavioural Decision Making.* Vol. 12, Issue 3 (September 1999), pp. 183–206.

20. Fayol, H. (1949). *General and industrial management.* London. Pitman and Sons, Ltd.

21. Bennett, N., & Lemoine, G. James (Jan–Feb 2014). What VUCA really means for you? *Harvard Business Review.* Vol. 92.

22. Dijksterhuis, Ap. (2004) Think different: the merits of unconscious thought in preference development and Decision Making. *Journal of Personality and Social Psychology.* Vol. 87, No. 5, 586–598. DOI: 10.1037/0022-3514.87.5.586.

23. Dwyer, C. (2017). Domain generality vs specificity. *Psychology Today.* https://www.psychologytoday.com/us/blog/thoughts-thinking/201711/domain-generality-vs-specificity.

24. Shadlen, M. N., & Shohamy, D. (2016). Decision making and sequential for memory. NCBI website: https://pubmed.ncbi.nlm.nih.gov/ Neuron. 1 June 2016; 90(5): 927–939. doi: 10.1016/j.neuron.2016.04.036.

25. Munger, C. (1995). The Psychology of Human Misjudgment. YouTube. https://www.youtube.com/watch?v=zNxsAhc6sk8.

26. Purcell, B.A, & Kiani, R. (2016). Neural mechanisms of post-error adjustments of decision policy in parietal cortex. *Neuron* 89 (3), 658-671.

27. History.com Editors (2020). Titanic. https://www.history.com/topics/early-20th-century-us/titanic.

28. Pugh, D. S., & Hickson, D. J. (2007). *Writers on organizations,* 6th edition. *Management and decision-making in organizations.* Chapter 3, pp 95-128. Newbury Park, California. SAGE Publishing. https://www.corwin.com/sites/default/files/upm-binaries/15500_Chapter_3.pdf.

29. Pugh, D. S, & Hickson, D. J. (2007). *Writers on organizations, 6th edition. Management and decision-making in organizations.* Chapter 3, pp 116. Newbury Park, California. SAGE Publishing. https://www.corwin.com/sites/default/files/upm-binaries/15500_Chapter_3.pdf.

30. Thaler, R. H. (2016). Behavioural economics: past, present and future. *American Economic Review 2016*, 106(7): 1577–1600.

31. McKenna, R.J., (1996). *Approaches to decision making.* Churchlands, Australia: Edith Cowan University. Retrieved from https://ro.ecu.edu.au/ecuworks/6811.

32. Klein, G. A. (1999). *Sources of Power. How People Make Decisions.* Massachusetts Institute of Technology. pp. 271.

33. Gino, F. (2016). What we miss when we judge the decision bythe outcome. *Harvard Business Review.* Retrieved from https://hbr.org/2016/09/what-we-miss-when-we-judge-a-decision-by-the-outcome.

34. Siegel-Jacobs, Karen, & Yates, J. F. (1996). Effects of procedural and outcome accountability on judgment quality. *Organizational Behaviour and Human Decision Processes*, 65(1), 1–17.

35. de Langhe, B., & Van Osselaer, S.M.J., & Wierenga, B. (2011). The effects of process and outcome accountability on judgment process and performance. *Organizational Behaviour and Human Decision Processes*, 115. 238-252. Retrieved from https://www.colorado.edu/business/sites/default/files/attached-files/obhdp_2011_de_langhe_van_osselaer_wierenga.pdf.

36. Barros, G.. (2010). Herbert A. Simon and the concept of rationality: Boundaries and procedures. *Brazilian Journal of Political Economy*, vol.30 no.3, pp. 455-472 Retrieved from https://doi.org/10.1590/S0101-31572010000300006.

37. Witzel, M. (2012). More luck than judgment. *Financial Times.* Retrieved from https://www.ft.com/content/e70e9292-1127-11e2-a637-00144feabdc0.

38. Wheeler, M. (2013). The luck factor in great decisions. *Harvard Business Review*. Retrieved from https://hbr.org/2013/11/the-luck-factor-in-great-decisions.

39. Taleb, N.N. (2010). *The Black Swan. The Impact of the Highly Improbable*. London. Penguin books.

40. Bazerman, M., & Moore, D. A. (2013). *Judgment in Managerial Decision Making*. 8th ed. Hoboken, New Jersey. John Wiley & Sons.

41. Deming, W.E. (2000). *Out of the crisis*. MIT Press.

42. Klein, G. (2011). *Streetlights and Shadows: Searching for the Keys to Adaptive Decision Making*. Bradford Books. MIT Press.

43. March, J. G. (1962). The business firm as a political coalition. *The Journal of Politics*, 24(4), 662-678. doi:10.2307/2128040

44. Klein, G. (2014) Management by discovery. *Psychology Today*. Retrieved from https://www.psychologytoday.com/us/blog/seeing-what-others-dont/201410/management-discovery.

45. Brent, G. (2000). *The Trumps: Three Generations of Builders and a President*. New York. Simon & Schuster.

46. Sunstein, C. R. (2001). Probability Neglect: Emotions, Worst Cases and Law. University of Chicago Law School.

47. Watkins, M. D. (June 2012). How managers become leaders. The seven seismic shifts of perspective and responsibility. *Harvard Business Review*.

48. Peter, L. J., & Hull, R. (1970). *The Peter Principle*. London. Pan Books edition.

49. Gosling, J, & Mintzberg, H. (2003). The five minds of a manager. *Harvard Business Review*. Retrieved from https://hbr.org/2003/11/the-five-minds-of-a-manager.

50. Chugh, D. (2004). Social and managerial implications of implicit social cognition: Why milliseconds matter. *Social Justice Research* 17 (7), 202-203.

51. Kahneman, D., Slovic, P., & Tversky, A., eds. (1982). *Judgment under uncertainty: Heuristics and biases.* Cambridge: Cambridge University Press. pp. 3–20.

52. Sammut-Bonnici, T., & Galea, D. (2015). *PEST analysis.* Wiley Online Library. Retrieved from 10.1002/9781118785317. weom120113.

53. Peter Todd, P, & Benbasat, I. (1992). The Use of Information in Decision Making: An Experimental Investigation of the Impact of Computer-Based Decision Aids. Management Information Systems Research Center, University of Minnesota. *MIS Quarterly,* Vol. 16, No. 3 (Sep., 1992), pp. 373-393.

54. Krogerus, M., & Tschappeler, R. (June 2016). How to make good decisions. TEDxDanubia.

55. Welch, S. (2009). *10-10-10: A life-transforming idea.* New York. Simon & Schuster.

56. Monahan, G. E. (2000). *Management Decision Making: Spreadsheet Modeling, Analysis, and Application.* Cambridge, UK; New York: Cambridge University Press.

57. Blenkom,M.W., Mankins, M., & Rogers, P. (June 2010). The decision-driven organization. *Harvard Business Review.*

58. De Smet, A., Jost, G., & Weiss, L. (May 2019). Three keys to faster, better decisions. *McKinsey Quarterly.*

59. Schuh, S. (2001). An evaluation of recent macroeconomic forecast errors. *New England Economic Review.*

60. Muraven M., & Baumeister R.F. (2000). Self-regulation and depletion of limited resources: Does self-control resemble a muscle? *Psychological Bulletin* https://doi.org/10.1037/0033-2909.126.2.247.

61. Danziger, S., Levav, J., & Avnaim-Pesso, L. (2011). Extraneous factors in judicial decisions. PNAS: *Proceedings of the National Academy of Sciences of the United States of America.* 26 April 2011. 108 (17) 6889-6892; Retrieved from https://doi.org/10.1073/pnas.1018033108.

62. Dobelli, R. (2013). *The Art Of Thinking Clearly*. New York. Harper Collins.

63. Taleb, N. N.(2007). *The Black Swan. The Impact of the Highly Improbable*. London. Penguin books.

64. Kruger, J., & Dunning, D. (1999). Unskilled and unaware of it: How difficulties in recognizing one's own incompetence lead to inflated self-assessments. *Journal of Personality and Social Psychology*, 77(6), 1121–1134.

65. Plous, S. (1993). *The Psychology of Judgment and Decision Making*. McGraw-Hill Education.

66. Buehler, R., Griffin, D., & Peetz, J. (2010). The planning fallacy: Cognitive, motivational, and social origins. *Advances in Experimental Social Psychology*. 43. pp. 1–62.

67. Oswald, M.E., & Grosjean, S. (2004). In Pohl RF (ed.). *Cognitive Illusions: A Handbook on Fallacies and Biases in Thinking, Judgement and Memory*. Hove, UK: Psychology Press. pp. 79–96.

68. Ericson, K. M. M., & Fuster, A. (2014). The endowment effect. *Annual Review of Economics*, 6(1), 555-579.

69. Kahneman, D. (2013). *Thinking, fast and slow*. New York. Penguin Books. pp. 283–286.

70. Olivola, C. Y. (2018). The interpersonal sunk-cost effect. *Psychological Science*. SAGE Journals.

71. Blanchette, I. (2010). The influence of affect on higher level cognition: A review of research on interpretation, judgement, decision making and reasoning. *Cognition and Emotion*. 24 (4): 561–595.

72. Cialdini, R. (1993). *Influence* (3rd ed.). New York: HarperCollins.

73. Reyna, V.F., Chick, C.F., Corbin, J.C.,& Hsia, A.N. (2014). Developmental reversals in risky decision-making: Intelligence agents show larger decision biases than college students. *Psychological Science*. 25 (1): 76)–84. doi:10.1177/0956797613497022.

74. Ngomane, M. (2019). *Everyday Ubutu. Living better together, the African way.* London. Bantam Press.

75. Hass, M., & Mortensen, M. (2016). The secrets of great teamwork. *Harvard Business Review,* June 2016, pp. 70-76.

76. De Morree, P. (2019). Beware: This hippo kills your company. Retrieved from www.corporate-rebels.com.

77. Ronstadt, R. (1988). *The art of case analysis.* Trafford, PA. Lord Publishing, Inc.

78. Yannis, N. (February 2017). The history of the case study at Harvard Business School. Harvard Business School online.

79. Klein, G. A. (1999). *Sources of Power. How People Make Decisions.* Massachusetts Institute of Technology. Pg. 30

80. Reed, E. S., Turiel, E., & Brown, T. (1996). *Values and Knowledge.* Abingdon, UK. Psychology Press. Taylor & Francis Group.

81. Halpern, D. F. (2014). *Thought and Knowledge. Introduction to Critical Thinking.* 5th ed. Abingdon, UK. Psychology Press. Taylor & Francis Group.

82. Molteni, M. (May 2021). *The 60-Year-Old Scientific Screwup That Helped Covid Kill.* WIRED. Retrieved from https://www.wired.com/story/the-teeny-tiny-scientific-screwup-that-helped-covid-kill/.

83. Evans, T. J. (November 1996). Deming's system of profound knowledge: An overview for international educators. ERIC – Institute of Education Sciences. Retrieved from https://files.eric.ed.gov/fulltext/ED401635.pdf.

84. Polanyi, M., & Sen, A. (2009). *The tacit dimension.* University of Chicago Press.

85. Reber, A. (1989). Implicit learning of tacit knowledge. *Journal of Experimental Psychology General* 118(3):219-235.

86. Granovetter, M. (1986). The strength of weak ties: A network theory revisited. Sociological Theory, Vol. 1. pp. 201-233.

87. Argandoña, A. (November 2015). Humility in Management. *Journal of Business Ethics* 132 (1): 63-71.

88. Imber, A. (July 2019). Timing is everything for good decision-making. New Zealand Management, August 2019.

89. Baron, J. (2004). Normative models of judgment and decision making. In D. J. Koehler & N. Harvey (Eds.), *Blackwell Handbook of Judgment and Decision Making*, pp. 19-36. London: Blackwell.

90. De Smet, A., Lackey, G. Weiss, L. M. (June 2017). Untangling your organization's decision making. *McKinsey Quarterly.*

91. Hyman, J. (October 2018). Why humble leaders make the best leaders. Forbes.com. Retrieved from https://www.forbes.com/sites/jeffhyman/2018/10/31/humility/?sh=247b3c7a1c80.